Meteor Design Patterns

Accelerate your code writing skills with over 20 programming patterns that will make your code easier to maintain and scale

Marcelo Reyna

BIRMINGHAM - MUMBAI

Meteor Design Patterns

First published: October 2015

Production reference: 1141015

Published by Packt Publishing Ltd.
Livery Place
35 Livery Street
Birmingham B3 2PB, UK.

ISBN 978-1-78398-762-7

www.packtpub.com

Credits

Author
Marcelo Reyna

Reviewers
Brad Cypert
Rohit Mukherjee
David Ryan Speer

Commissioning Editor
Pramila Balan

Acquisition Editor
Tushar Gupta

Content Development Editor
Adrian Raposo

Technical Editor
Tanmayee Patil

Copy Editor
Kausambhi Majumdar

Project Coordinator
Kinjal Bari

Proofreader
Safis Editing

Indexer
Tejal Soni

Production Coordinator
Aparna Bhagat

Cover Work
Aparna Bhagat

About the Author

Marcelo Reyna is an industrial engineer and a fellow business owner (RetroSoda LLC). While building his company, he realized many business processes could be automated, which is when he decided to take up programming full time. As soon as he realized that programming is his passion, he dedicated 3 years to deeply understand all the aspects of the Meteor framework and how to take web applications built on this into production. Today, he is an avid programmer involved in the technology start-up scene.

I would like to thank Packt Publishing's team, Llewellyn Rozario, Tushar Gupta, and Adrian Raposo, for giving me the opportunity to write this book. Also, I would like to thank David Ryan Speer and Rohit Mukherjee for their invaluable feedback. I thank my older brother, Reynaldo Reyna Jr, and my father, Reynaldo Reyna, for helping me build RetroSoda 3 years ago; without RetroSoda, I would have never invested so much time in learning how to program. Also, I thank my mother, Elsa Mireya Vazquez, for her constant support in my endeavors and my fiancée, Eugenia Perez, for giving me a reason to accomplish greater goals.

About the Reviewers

Brad Cypert is a frontend-focused web developer with a year and a half of Meteor experience. He has previously worked for CARFAX and currently, works for LinkedIn. In his spare time, he writes Ember apps or gives conference talks on frontend technology.

Rohit Mukherjee works as a software engineer at SigFig, based in San Francisco and Singapore. He works mostly on Scala and Java backend services. He graduated with a bachelor's degree in computer engineering from The National University of Singapore (NUS) and has also spent some time in ETH Zurich studying graduate courses in computer science.

He has experience of working in financial software, technical publishing, and healthcare technology, and enjoys finding his way through the stack. He is passionate about Agile methodologies and continuous delivery.

He has worked for Bank of America, Merrill Lynch Singapore, ETH Zurich, Klinify Singapore, and SigFig, Singapore and San Francisco.

I would like to thank my parents and Pratish Mondal for their support.

David Ryan Speer is a web designer and Meteor developer based in Los Angeles, California. He creates applications and websites for small-to-medium-sized companies, non-profit organizations, and for in-office use. With over 10 years of experience in PHP and MySQL development, he and his team completely switched to Meteor development because of its ease of use and rapid development capability. With Meteor, David has created fast and reactive applications in the energy, education, and non-profit sectors.

I would like to thank Lynn, Maxx, and Parker for their continuous love and support, my dad for his analytical and thoughtful mind, my mom for her patience and endless encouragement, and my siblings, Colleen and Jordan, for their boundless creativity.

www.PacktPub.com

Support files, eBooks, discount offers, and more

For support files and downloads related to your book, please visit www.PacktPub.com.

Did you know that Packt offers eBook versions of every book published, with PDF and ePub files available? You can upgrade to the eBook version at www.PacktPub.com and as a print book customer, you are entitled to a discount on the eBook copy. Get in touch with us at service@packtpub.com for more details.

At www.PacktPub.com, you can also read a collection of free technical articles, sign up for a range of free newsletters and receive exclusive discounts and offers on Packt books and eBooks.

https://www2.packtpub.com/books/subscription/packtlib

Do you need instant solutions to your IT questions? PacktLib is Packt's online digital book library. Here, you can search, access, and read Packt's entire library of books.

Why subscribe?

- Fully searchable across every book published by Packt
- Copy and paste, print, and bookmark content
- On demand and accessible via a web browser

Free access for Packt account holders

If you have an account with Packt at www.PacktPub.com, you can use this to access PacktLib today and view 9 entirely free books. Simply use your login credentials for immediate access.

Table of Contents

Preface

Simplicity is the shortest path to a solution. Meteor is a web development framework that simplifies programming and once it is mastered, gives the developer the power to prototype applications in just a few days and build a production app in just a few weeks. The simplicity of the framework makes maintenance a breeze as well; reorganizing and renaming files will not break your code, code is easy to keep in modules, and virtual environments are a thing of the past. The Meteor Development Group has established the shortest path for web development by producing a feature-rich framework that takes all the experience learned from other frameworks and packs it into Meteor.

While Meteor is simple because of the technical features it comes packed with, it is clear that the framework will become the status quo because of how the team behind it works. Meteor is built by a team that has been actively funded since the beginning of the project, unlike many open source frameworks such as Ruby on Rails, Laravel, CakePHP, and others. This means that the people working towards building the framework actually care about it. Yet, Meteor is an open source project with an active community that has been improving the project constantly through packages or by patching the core code

What this book covers

Chapter 1, *Getting Started with Meteor*, covers the basics of Meteor web development. It will cover programming in the same languages (CoffeeScript, Stylus, and Jade), teach us about templates, helpers, and events, and show how to structure web applications.

Chapter 2, *Publish and Subscribe Patterns*, covers the most important part of Meteor web development—publishers and subscribers. With this chapter, you will understand how to better organize your data to publish only the information that the client requires.

Chapter 3, Front-end Patterns, covers a handful of patterns to improve your frontend code. You will learn how to keep code from repeating and keep it modular, use different kinds of variables, create custom input elements, animations, and more.

Chapter 4, Application Patterns, covers more complex patterns that help to control how data flows into the client, how to keep this data secure, and how to connect with external APIs.

Chapter 5, Testing Patterns, covers how to maintain your code. You will learn how to test all the features of the application and how to only test functions. This will ensure that your code does not break when you start moving things around in the future.

Chapter 6, Deployment, covers how to bring your application to a production environment that will work the way it is meant to work. You will learn how to activate the oplog, how to track errors, and how to set up an SSL certificate.

What you need for this book

- Meteor version 1.1.0.2 or above
- A Unix system such as a Mac or Linux computer

Who this book is for

This book is for developers who have already had an introductory course with Meteor. A basic knowledge of web development is recommended.

Conventions

In this book, you will find a number of text styles that distinguish between different kinds of information. Here are some examples of these styles and an explanation of their meaning.

Code words in text, database table names, folder names, filenames, file extensions, pathnames, dummy URLs, user input, and Twitter handles are shown as follows: "We are using font awesome to create some icons for our `#features` section as well."

A block of code is set as follows:

```
@import "_globals/bootstrap/custom.bootstrap.import.styl"

#products
  #promoter
    background: $brand-primary
```

```
    height: 80%

@import "_globals/bootstrap/custom.bootstrap.import.styl"

#products
  #promoter
    background: $brand-primary
    height: 80%
```

When we wish to draw your attention to a particular part of a code block, the relevant lines or items are set in bold:

// /_globals/client/main.styl

```
html, body, #__flow-root, #__flow-root > .template
  height:100%
```

Any command-line input or output is written as follows:

```
meteor reset
```

New terms and **important words** are shown in bold. Words that you see on the screen, for example, in menus or dialog boxes, appear in the text like this: "Paste the information to the **Private Key** textarea."

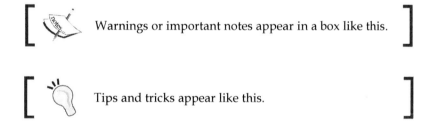

Warnings or important notes appear in a box like this.

Tips and tricks appear like this.

Reader feedback

Feedback from our readers is always welcome. Let us know what you think about this book—what you liked or disliked. Reader feedback is important for us as it helps us develop titles that you will really get the most out of.

To send us general feedback, simply e-mail feedback@packtpub.com, and mention the book's title in the subject of your message.

If there is a topic that you have expertise in and you are interested in either writing or contributing to a book, see our author guide at www.packtpub.com/authors.

Customer support

Now that you are the proud owner of a Packt book, we have a number of things to help you to get the most from your purchase.

Downloading the example code

You can download the example code files from your account at `http://www.packtpub.com` for all the Packt Publishing books you have purchased. If you purchased this book elsewhere, you can visit `http://www.packtpub.com/support` and register to have the files e-mailed directly to you.

Errata

Although we have taken every care to ensure the accuracy of our content, mistakes do happen. If you find a mistake in one of our books—maybe a mistake in the text or the code—we would be grateful if you could report this to us. By doing so, you can save other readers from frustration and help us improve subsequent versions of this book. If you find any errata, please report them by visiting `http://www.packtpub.com/submit-errata`, selecting your book, clicking on the **Errata Submission Form** link, and entering the details of your errata. Once your errata are verified, your submission will be accepted and the errata will be uploaded to our website or added to any list of existing errata under the Errata section of that title.

To view the previously submitted errata, go to `https://www.packtpub.com/books/content/support` and enter the name of the book in the search field. The required information will appear under the **Errata** section.

Piracy

Piracy of copyrighted material on the Internet is an ongoing problem across all media. At Packt, we take the protection of our copyright and licenses very seriously. If you come across any illegal copies of our works in any form on the Internet, please provide us with the location address or website name immediately so that we can pursue a remedy.

Please contact us at `copyright@packtpub.com` with a link to the suspected pirated material.

We appreciate your help in protecting our authors and our ability to bring you valuable content.

Questions

If you have a problem with any aspect of this book, you can contact us at questions@packtpub.com, and we will do our best to address the problem.

1
Getting Started with Meteor

Meteor is a framework that is essentially fast for the purpose of development even if you program at a slow pace. The aim of this book is to increase your development speed and improve quality. There are two key ingredients required to improve development: compilers and patterns. Compilers add functionality to your coding language, while patterns increase the speed at which you solve common programming issues.

This book will mostly cover patterns, but we'll use this chapter to quick start compilers and understand how they relate to Meteor—a vast but simple topic. The compilers that we will look at are as follows:

- CoffeeScript
- Jade
- Stylus

We will review some basic knowledge you should have about Meteor. This will cover the following:

- Templates, helpers, and events
- The event loop and the merge box
- The must-have packages
- Folder structure

CoffeeScript for Meteor

CoffeeScript is a compiler for JavaScript that adds "syntactic sugar" inspired by Ruby, Python, and Haskell; it effectively makes the writing of JavaScript easier and more readable. CoffeeScript simplifies the syntax of functions, objects, arrays, logical statements, binding, managing scope, and much more. All CoffeeScript files are saved with a .coffee extension. We will cover functions, objects, logical statements, and bindings as these are some of the most commonly used features.

Objects and arrays

CoffeeScript gets rid of curly braces ({ }), semicolons (;), and commas (,). This alone saves you from repeating unnecessary strokes on the keyboard. Instead, CoffeeScript emphasizes on the proper use of **tabbing**. Tabbing will not only make your code more readable, but it will be a key factor in making the code work as well. In fact, you are probably already tabbing the right way! Let's look at some examples:

```
#COFFEESCRIPT
toolbox =
  hammer:true
  flashlight:false
```

Downloading the example code

You can download the example code files from your account at http://www.packtpub.com for all the Packt Publishing books you have purchased. If you purchased this book elsewhere, you can visit http://www.packtpub.com/support and register to have the files e-mailed directly to you.

Here, we are creating an object named toolbox that contains two keys: hammer and flashlight. The equivalent in JavaScript will be this:

```
//JAVASCRIPT - OUTPUT
var toolbox = {
  hammer:true,
  flashlight:false
};
```

Much easier! As you can see, we have to **tab** to indicate that both the `hammer` and `flashlight` properties are a part of `toolbox`. The `var` word is not allowed in CoffeeScript because CoffeeScript automatically applies it for you. Let's have a look at how we would make an array:

```
#COFFEESCRIPT
drill_bits = [
  "1/16 in"
  "5/64 in"
  "3/32 in"
  "7/64 in"
]
```

```
//JAVASCRIPT - OUTPUT
var drill_bits;
drill_bits = ["1/16 in","5/64 in","3/32 in","7/64 in"];
```

Here, we can see that we don't need to have any commas, but we do need to have brackets to determine that this is an array.

Logical statements and operators

CoffeeScript removes a lot of parenthesis (()) in logical statements and functions as well. This makes the logic of the code much easier to understand at first glance. Let's look at an example:

```
#COFFEESCRIPT
rating = "excellent" if five_star_rating
```

```
//JAVASCRIPT - OUTPUT
var rating;

if(five_star_rating){
  rating = "excellent";
}
```

In this example, we can clearly see that CoffeeScript is easier to read and write. CoffeeScript effectively replaces the entire **implied parenthesis** in any logical statement.

Operators such as `&&`, `||`, and `!==` are replaced by words to make the code more readable. Here is a list of the operators that you will be using the most:

CoffeeScript	JavaScript
`is`	`===`
`isnt`	`!==`
`not`	`!`
`and`	`&&`
`or`	`||`
`true, yes, on`	`true`
`false, no, off`	`false`
`@, this`	`this`

Let's look at a slightly more complex logical statement and see how it is compiled:

```
#COFFEESCRIPT
# Suppose that "this" is an object that represents a person and
their physical properties

if @eye_color is "green"
  retina_scan = "passed"
else
  retina_scan = "failed"
```

```
//JAVASCRIPT - OUTPUT
if(this.eye_color === "green"){
  retina_scan = "passed";
} else {
  retina_scan = "failed";
}
```

Notice how the context of `this` is passed to the `@` symbol without the need for a period, making `@eye_color` equal to `this.eye_color`.

Functions

A JavaScript function is a block of code designed to perform a particular task. JavaScript has a couple of ways of creating functions that are simplified in CoffeeScript. They look like this:

```
//JAVASCRIPT
//Save an anonymous function onto a variable
var hello_world = function(){
```

```
    console.log("Hello World!");
}

//Declare a function
function hello_world(){
    console.log("Hello World!");
}
```

CoffeeScript uses `->` instead of the `function()` keyword. The following example outputs a `hello_world` function:

```
#COFFEESCRIPT
#Create a function
hello_world = ->
    console.log "Hello World!"

//JAVASCRIPT - OUTPUT
var hello_world;
hello_world = function(){
    return console.log("Hello World!");
}
```

Once again, we will use a tab to specify the contents of the function so that there is no need for curly braces ({ }). This means that you have to make sure that you have the entire logic of the function tabbed under its namespace.

What about our parameters? We can use `(p1,p2) ->` where p1 and p2 are parameters. Let's make our `hello_world` function output our name:

```
#COFFEESCRIPT
hello_world = (name) ->
    console.log "Hello #{name}"

//JAVSCRIPT - OUTPUT
var hello_world;
hello_world = function(name) {
    return console.log("Hello " + name);
}
```

In this example, we can see how parameters are placed inside parentheses. We are also doing **string interpolation**. CoffeeScript allows the programmer to easily add logic to a string by escaping the string with #{ }. Also notice that, unlike JavaScript, you do not have to return anything at the end of the function, CoffeeScript automatically returns the output of the last command.

Binding

In Meteor, we will often find ourselves using the properties of `this` within nested functions and callbacks. **Function binding** is very useful for these types of cases and helps to avoid saving data in additional variables. Function binding sets the value of the `this` object inside the function to the value of `this` outside the function. Let's look at an example:

```
#COFFEESCRIPT
# Let's make the context of this equal to our toolbox object
# this =
#   hammer:true
#   flashlight:false


# Run a method with a callback
Meteor.call "use_hammer", ->
  console.log this
```

In this case, the `this` object will return a top-level object such as the browser window. This is not useful at all. Let's bind `this` now:

```
#COFFEESCRIPT
# Let's make the context of this equal to our toolbox object
# this =
#   hammer:true
#   flashlight:false


# Run a method with a callback
Meteor.call "use_hammer", =>
  console.log this
```

The key difference is the use of `=>` instead of the expected `->` to define the function. Using `=>` will make the callback's `this` object equal to the context of the executing function. The resulting compiled script is as follows:

```
//JAVASCRIPT
Meteor.call("use_hammer", (function(_this) {
  return function() {
    return Console.log(_this);
  };
})(this));
```

CoffeeScript will improve your coding quality and speed. Still, *CoffeeScript is not flawless*. When you start combining functions with nested arrays, things can get complex and difficult to read, especially when the functions are constructed with multiple parameters. Let's look at a common query that does not look as readable as you would expect it to be:

```
#COFFEESCRIPT
People.update
  sibling:
    $in:["bob","bill"]
  ,
  limit:1
  ->
    console.log "success!"
```

This collection query is passing three parameters: the `filter` object, the `options` object, and the callback function. To differentiate between the first two objects, we had to place a comma at the same level as the function and then, indent the second parameter. This is unwieldy, but we can use variables in order to make the query more readable:

```
#COFFEESCRIPT
filter =
  sibling:
    $in:["bob","bill"]
options =
  limit:1
People.update filter, options, ->
  console.log "success!"
```

Go to `coffeescript.org` and play around with the language by clicking on the "try coffeescript" link.

Jade for Meteor

Jade works much like CoffeeScript but it is used for HTML instead. I recommend that you install the `mquandalle:jade` package. All the Jade files are saved with a `.jade` extension. This section will cover the most used aspects of Jade in Meteor such as HTML tags, components, and helpers.

HTML tags

Much like CoffeeScript, Jade is a language that depends heavily on tabbing. When you want to add children to an HTML tag, you simply use tab. Tag IDs and classes can be added using the CSS selector notation (`'input#name.first'`). This means classes are expressed with a dot (`.`) and IDs are expressed with a pound (#). Let's look at an example:

```
//- JADE
div#container
  ul.list
    li(data-bind="clickable") Click me!
```

```
<!-- HTML - OUTPUT -->
<div id="container">
  <ul class="list">
    <li data-bind="clickable">Click me!</li>
  </ul>
</div>
```

As you can see, **special** attributes such as `data-bind` are added with parenthesis. Symbols such as `<`, `>`, and **closures** are not required anymore. In this example, we have a `div` tag with an `id` attribute of `"container"`, a `ul` tag with a `class` attribute of list, and a `li` tag with a special attribute of `data-bind`.

You will find yourself using special attributes often for the `input` tags to add `value`, `placeholder`, and other attributes.

Templates and components

Meteor templates are Jade components. In Meteor, we define a template with the template tag and apply the special `name` attribute to create a reusable HTML block. In Jade, when we create a template, we create a component as well. This looks as follows:

```
//- JADE
template(name="landing")
  h3 Hello World!
```

```
<!-- HTML - OUTPUT -->
<template name="landing">
  <h3>Hello World!</h3>
</template>
```

Now we can use this template as a Jade component anywhere in our views. To call a Jade component, you simply prepend a plus sign to the name of the template. Let's look at an example where we want to place a `landing` page inside a `main_layout` page:

```
//- JADE
template(name="landing")
  h3 Hello World!

template(name="main_layout")
  +landing
```

```
<!-- HTML - OUTPUT -->
<template name="landing">
  <h3>Hello World!</h3>
</template>

<template name="main_layout">
  {{> landing}}
</template>
```

That's it! Notice that we have prepended the plus (+) sign to the name of the template to call it. This is equivalent to using `{{> landing}}` in SpaceBars (Meteor's version of Handlebars). Components can have parameters as well, which can be later used in the templates' instance. Let's make our example output someone's name:

```
//- JADE
template(name="landing")
  h3 Hello {{name}}

template(name="main_layout")
  +landing(name="Mr Someone")
```

```
# COFFEESCRIPT
Template.landing.helpers
  "name": ->
    Template.instance().data.name
```

```
<!-- HTML - OUTPUT -->
<template name="landing">
  <h3>Hello {{name}}</h3>
</template>

<template name="main_layout">
  {{> landing name="Mr Someone"}}
</template>
```

Adding attributes to your templates can make your templates flexible as shown in the preceding example. Still, it is unlikely that you will have to use this as templates "soak up" data from their parent context.

Helpers

Helpers in Meteor are functions that return data before rendering to the view. We use helpers for iteration, logical statements, and variables. The two basic helpers are `each` and `if`, but adding the `raix:handlebar-helpers` package will add a dictionary of other useful helpers to keep your code from repeating. Let's have a look at how we can use our helpers:

```
//- JADE
template(name="list_of_things")
  each things
    if selected
      p.selected {{name}}
    else
      p {{name}}
```

```
<!-- HTML - OUTPUT -->
<template name="list_of_things">
  {{#each things}}
    {{#if selected}}
      <p class="selected">{{name}}</p>
    {{else}}
      <p>{{name}}</p>
    {{/if}}
  {{/each}}
</template>
```

In this example, the `each` helper is iterating through the return value of another helper named `things` and if the `selected` helper resolves to `true`, then we will render `p.selected` with the `name` variable.

It's important to understand that everything that is not an HTML tag is a helper, and that if you want to use a helper within a tag, you need to use {{}} or #{} to express this.

Go to `jade-lang.com` and `handlebars.js` to know more specific information. With this information, you should be able to do just about anything.

Stylus for Meteor

Stylus works much like CoffeeScript and Jade but it is for CSS. I recommend that you install `mquandalle:stylus`. This package is preinstalled with useful tools such as `Jeet` and `Rupture`. All Stylus files are saved with a `.styl` extension. There are only three things that we need to learn about Stylus: CSS tags, variables, and functions.

CSS tags

Stylus is a language that does away with the need for semicolons (`;`) and curly braces (`{}`) in exchange for making good use of tabbing. Let's look at an example:

```
// STYLUS
// Let's make a vertical positioning class
.vertical-align-middle
  //PART 1
  position:absolute
  width:100%
  height:100%
  display:table
  overflow-x:hidden


  .special
    background:black
```

We can see in `PART 1` how properties are defined for a class by tabbing those properties in `.special` is used to select an HTML tag with the `special` class that is a child of the `vertical-align-middle` class. Let's look at how `PART 1` compiles:

```
/* CSS - OUTPUT PART 1 */
.vertical-align-middle {
  position:absolute;
  width:100%;
  height:100%;
  display:table;
  overflow-x:hidden;
}
.vertical-align-middle .special {
  background:black;
}
```

Now let's add a more complex selector:

```
// STYLUS
// Let's make a vertical positioning class
.vertical-align-middle
  //PART 1
  ...

  //PART 2
  > *
    display:table-cell
    vertical-align:middle
```

PART 2 has a combination of special CSS2 selectors: specific parent (>) and all elements (*). In this particular order, the CSS2 selectors are picking the "any first sibling" element only and applying the rules. Let's look at how PART 2 compiles:

```
/* CSS - OUTPUT PART 2 */
.vertical-align-middle > * {
  display:table-cell;
  vertical-align:middle;
}
```

Let's add a new class to the current class that aligns the object to the top:

```
// STYLUS
// Let's make a vertical positioning class
.vertical-align-middle
  //PART 1
  ...
  //PART 2
  ...
  //PART 3
  &.whole-page
    top:0
```

PART 3 uses an ampersand (&) to describe an element that is not a child but instead is concatenated with the extra class. Let's look at how PART 3 compiles:

```
/* CSS - OUTPUT PART 3 */
.vertical-align-middle.whole-page {
  top:0;
}
```

Variables

Unlike CSS, Stylus supports variables. This keeps a lot of things manageable when we want to make major changes to the look of our site. Suppose we have two colors that we want to use throughout our site, but we know that these colors are going to change. Let's define them as variables so that we can easily modify them later:

```
// STYLUS
primary-color = #ffffff
$secondary-color = #333333

.text-default
  color:primary-color
  background:$secondary-color

.text-inverted
  color:$secondary-color
  background:primary-color
```

Easy right? In this example, both `primary-color` and `$secondary-color` are variables. Stylus optionally supports the use of the money sign ($) to indicate a variable. This can make it easier to spot variables.

Functions/mixins

Unlike CSS, Stylus supports functions too. LESS, Stylus, and **Sassy CSS (SCSS)** refer to functions as **mixins**. Functions will make your CSS concoctions much easier to share across a project. We will cover the two types of mixins in Stylus: mixins and transparent mixins.

Mixins are functions that take a defined set of parameters. Let's take a look at how we can write a mixin:

```
// STYLUS
animation(duration,delay,timing)
  -webkit-animation-duration:duration
  animation-duration:duration
  -webkit-animation-delay:delay
  animation-delay:delay
  -webkit-animation-timing-function:timing
  animation-timing-function:timing

button
  animation(500ms,0,ease-out)
```

```
/* CSS - OUTPUT */
button {
  -webkit-animation-duration:500ms;
  animation-duration:500ms;
  -webkit-animation-delay:0;
  animation-delay:0;
  -webkit-animation-timing-function:ease-out;
  animation-timing-function:ease-out;
}
```

In this example, we first define the `animation` mixin, and then we apply the mixin to the `button` HTML tag. However, there is a much easier and effective way of doing this via a transparent mixin.

A transparent mixin, basically, takes all the parameters and saves them in an `arguments` variable without you having to define anything. Let's have a look:

```
// STYLUS
animation()
  -webkit-animation:arguments
  animation:arguments

button
  animation(pulse 3s ease infinite)
```

```
/* CSS - OUTPUT */
button {
  -webkit-animation:pulse 3s ease infinite;
  animation:pulse 3s ease infinite;
}
```

Notice how we did not have to define every single parameter in the mixin, and the `arguments` variable simply passed all the arguments that it could find. This is especially useful for keeping the code flexible.

Stylus essentially upgrades CSS in such a way that it makes the code much easier to manage and therefore, ends up saving us a lot of development time.

Go to `stylus-lang.com` and `learnboost.github.io/stylus` to learn more about Stylus.

Templates, helpers, and events

Now that we are on the same page for the languages that we are going to use throughout the book, let's do a quick review of some of the elements that we will use during our development process.

Templates, helpers, and events are used to build the frontend of your application. Using them effectively is the key to how we design our backend as well (which we will address in *Chapter 2, Publish and Subscribe Patterns*).

Templates

Meteor templates are the special blocks of HTML code that generate Meteor template objects (`Template.<yourtemplate>`). It is through Meteor template objects that we wire the HTML code to logic. People who have worked with an MVC framework will refer to these templates as views. This is a key concept to understand.

Open up your terminal and create a new project:

`meteor create basic_meteor`

Now let's add our languages:

`meteor add coffeescript`

`meteor add mquandalle:jade`

`meteor add mquandalle:stylus`

Remove the three visible files from `/basic_meteor` (do not remove any of the files starting with a dot), and create `/client/layout.jade`. This is something that exists in one way or another in every Meteor project. Let's program:

```
//- layout.jade
head
  title Meteor Basics
  meta(name="viewport" content="user-scalable=no, initial-
  scale=1.0, maximum-scale=1.0")
  meta(name="apple-mobile-web-app-capable" content="yes")
body
  +basic_template
```

I highly recommend adding these metatags to make your site mobile-friendly right from the beginning. With this snippet of code, we are effectively starting up the very first thing that Meteor is going to render before running any code. Once this is rendered, Jade takes care of rendering `basic_template`. Let's program this in a new file, `/client/basic_template.jade`:

```
//- basic_template.jade
template(name="basic_template")
  h1 Hello World!
```

Behind the scenes, Meteor is compiling our Jade templates and putting them all in one big file. You will never have to worry about loading `basic_template.jade` before `layout.jade` when it comes to templating.

Throughout the book, we will use `meteorhacks:flow-router` and `meteorhacks:flow-layout` to easily navigate to different templates.

Creating helpers

We have already discussed what helpers are in Jade, but how do we create helpers in Meteor? Let's go back to our `basic_meteor` project and create `/client/basic_template.coffee`. It is important to understand that Meteor helpers are used to control the variables in our template. People who have worked with an MVC framework can view this file as a controller. Let's write our first helper:

```
#basic_template.coffee
Template.basic_template.helpers
  "name": ->
    "Mr Someone"
```

Notice that the helper is defined within the `helpers` function of the Meteor template object: `Template.<your_template>.helpers(<your_helpers>)`. Helpers are mostly functions that will return anything you want them to including Meteor collection cursors. Let's bring all this together now:

```
//- basic_template.jade
template(name="basic_template")
  h1 Hello {{name}}
```

This will output `Hello Mr Someone` inside the `h1` HTML tag. Let's add a slightly more complex helper:

```
#basic_template.coffee
Template.basic_template.helpers
  "person": ->
    name:"Someone"
```

```
     prefix: "Mr"
     children: [
       {
         name:"Billy"
       }
       {
         name:"Nancy"
       }
     ]


//- basic_template.jade
template(name="basic_template")
  with person
    h1 Hello {{prefix}} {{name}}

    ul
      each children
        li {{name}}
```

In this example, we are using `with` to set up the **data context** of the HTML tags that belong to it; this data context is equivalent to `person`. Data context refers to the value of `this` inside a helper. So if you set up an object as the data context, `this` will be equivalent to that object. Also, we iterate through `children` with an `each` statement so that we can list out their names.

Events

Meteor taps into common JavaScript HTML events such as click, change, and focus. An event is anything that happens to an HTML element that you are listening to. Suppose we want to be able to change the name of a person to one of the children by clicking on them. We do this through the templates' event map. Let's take a look at an example of how we can do this without using reactivity or collections:

```
#basic_template.coffee
Template.basic_template.events
  "click li": ->
    $("h1").text "Hello #{@name}"
```

Easy! So to catch template events, we need to use the `Template.<your_template>.events(<your_event_map>)` function. In this particular example, we are using jQuery to replace text.

The `event map` is an object where the properties specify a set of events to be handled. These events may be specified in any of the following ways:

```
# Runs any time you click anywhere
"click": ->

# Runs any time you click a li element
"click li": ->

#Runs any time you click a li element OR mouseover a li element
"click li, mouseover li": ->
```

The key `string` of the event is composed of two parts: the first is always a type of event (click, hover, change, and so on) while the second is always a CSS selector.

The event loop and the merge box

Before diving into Meteor, it is critical to understand what the event loop and the merge box are and how they can adversely affect your code. Both are relatively complex in the way that they were programmed, so we will focus on understanding the general concept.

The event loop

The event loop is like a queue; it runs a series of functions one by one. Because functions are processed sequentially, each function effectively blocks others from being processed until the function is done.

In other words, the event loop functions much like a single-line conveyor belt where things are being inspected. For every inspection made, the line is stopped and nothing moves.

Meteor uses Fibers – a NodeJS library – to get around this issue. Many of the functions that you will run will be on a separate fiber. What does this mean? This means that the functions will run on a separate conveyor belt for processing. Still, not all functions are built this way, you need to make sure your server-side functions do not block the server.

So which functions could potentially cause the server to get blocked? `Meteor.methods()`, `Meteor.publish()`, and `any` function that does not run inside a fiber on the server. Let's see how we can unblock each one and when we should do this.

Functions defined under the `Meteor.methods()` that you know are going to take a long time to process, should always run on a Fiber or defer time consuming code to a Fiber. We can quickly solve this by calling the `@unblock()` function from within the method. Let's look at an example:

```
# METEOR METHODS
Meteor.methods
  #BLOCKING
  time_consuming: ->
    Meteor.setTimeout ->
        console.log "done"
      ,60000

  #NON-BLOCKING
  time_consuming_unblock: ->
    @unblock()
    Meteor.setTimeout ->
        console.log "done"
      ,60000
```

In this example, when you run `Meteor.call("time_consuming")`, the server will be blocked. When the server is blocked, other visitors won't be able to reach your site! Instead if you run `Meteor.call("time_consuming_unblock")`, the server will continue to function properly but consume more resources to do so.

`Meteor.publish()` can be easily unblocked after installing the `meteorhacks:unblock` package as well. This one will be particularly useful when we start to make very complex publishers that might consume a lot of resources. Let's look at an example:

```
# METEOR PUBLISH
#BLOCKING
Meteor.publish "external_API_query", ->
  HTTP.get "http://connect.square.com/payments"

#NON-BLOCKING
Meteor.publish "external_API_query_unblocked", ->
  @unblock()
  HTTP.get "http://connect.square.com/payments"
```

In this example, we are waiting for an HTTP call to respond. This will certainly block the server if we subscribe to `external_API_query`, so we use `external_API_query_unblocked` instead.

All other functions that run on the server and you know are going to block the server, should run on a fiber. Meteor has a special function to help us make this easy. It is called `Meteor.wrapAsync()`. Let's see how this works:

```
# METEOR UNBLOCKED FUNCTION
unblock_me = Meteor.wrapAsync ->
  Meteor.setTimeout ->
      console.log "done"
    ,60000
```

 It is very important to keep the event loop in mind, especially when we're connecting our web application to external services that are going to cause massive delays to our server.

The merge box

The merge box is the algorithm that identifies all the changes that are happening to the database. It basically handles publishers, subscribers, and reactivity. The merge box also handles the initial load of data using DDP messages.

It is important to understand that we can communicate directly with the merge box via all the commands that are available to us under the `Meteor.publish()` function. The more optimal we can make our `Meteor.publish` functions, the faster the site will load.

The beginning of our online shop

Throughout the book we will be developing an e-commerce website to help us understand the core concepts of advanced Meteor web development. Let's begin by creating a new project:

```
meteor create online_shop
```

The must-have packages

`Atmospherejs.com` has always been the "go to" website to find packages. Here you will find thousands of packages produced by the community for free. There are a handful of packages that we absolutely need to install to make our website function properly.

First, we install the languages:

```
meteor add coffeescript
meteor add mquandalle:jade
meteor add mquandalle:stylus
meteor add less
```

Next, the router and functions that will help us with SEO and routing:

```
meteor add kadira:flow-router
meteor add kadira:blaze-layout
meteor add meteorhacks:fast-render
meteor add nimble:restivus
meteor add yasinuslu:blaze-meta
meteor add dfischer:prerenderio
meteor add wizonesolutions:canonical
```

 WARNING: Do not run Meteor yet! Canonical could mess up your project unless you have it set up correctly.

We will need a couple of packages as well to help us manage publishers:

```
meteor add lepozepo:publish-with-relations
meteor add tmeasday:publish-counts
meteor add meteorhacks:aggregate
meteor add http
meteor add meteorhacks:unblock
```

These next packages will extend Meteor's functions:

```
meteor add xorax:multiple-callbacks
meteor add aldeed:collection2
meteor add aldeed:autoform
meteor add fastclick
meteor add reactive-var
meteor add alanning:roles
meteor add accounts-password

meteor add u2622:persistent-session
meteor add ongoworks:security
```

We will need these packages to properly manage time:

```
meteor add momentjs:moment
meteor add mrt:moment-timezone
```

For the last set, we'll be using a couple of additional packages that will make the design process much faster:

```
meteor add kyleking:customizable-bootstrap-stylus
meteor add raix:handlebar-helpers
meteor add fortawesome:fontawesome

meteor add percolate:momentum
```

We need to remove some packages for security too:

```
meteor remove autopublish
meteor remove insecure
```

All of these packages will be explained in more detail throughout the book, but all of these are must-haves. The first package that we need to explain is the `wizonesolutions:canonical` package. This package makes sure that all incoming traffic is routed to your ROOT_URL, so it is particularly useful when you want all the traffic to go to your SSL site. The first thing that we need to do before running Meteor is set up canonical to run only in the production environment.

Create `/server/canonical.coffee`, and add this code:

```
#/server/canonical.coffee
if process.env.NODE_ENV is "development" or
process.env.ROOT_URL.indexOf("meteor.com") > -1
  Meteor.startup ->
    process.env.PACKAGE_CANONICAL_DISABLE = true
```

This code snippet effectively sets your PACKAGE_CANONICAL_DISABLE environment variable to make sure that canonical is inactive while you are developing.

What are environment variables? These variables are defined within the scope of the deployment, and they make sure that the project knows information before the build finishes on the server. Information such as what database to use, which domains to use, and other setup information can usually be found in these variables. We will cover this information in the final chapter.

File structure

A proper file structure is tremendously important in Meteor. We have found that the best way to work is with functional top-level modules. This means that every folder is a micro-service, and therefore can act on its own. This allows for a lot of modularity in the project, and it's very easy for others to understand what it is that you are trying to accomplish. In this section, we will cover this file structure and Meteor's special folders.

Let's look at a sample web application folder structure:

```
/online_shop
/online_shop/cart
/online_shop/cart/cart_route.coffee   #RUNS ON CLIENT AND SERVER
/online_shop/cart/client
/online_shop/cart/client/cart_view.jade   #RUNS ON CLIENT ONLY
/online_shop/cart/client/cart_controller.coffee
/online_shop/cart/client/cart.styl
/online_shop/cart/server
/online_shop/cart/server/cart_publisher.coffee   #RUNS ON SERVER
ONLY
/online_shop/cart/server/cart_methods.coffee
```

In this folder structure, `cart` is the micro-service, and it is composed of a route, view, controller, and publisher. The files placed under a `/client` directory will be published to the client and will only run on the client. The files placed under a `/server` directory will only run and be accessible on the server. If a file is placed in none of these directories, then the file will run on both the client and server. The expected structure goes like this:

```
/project_folder
/project_folder/_globals
   ./client/<global support function files>
   ./server/<global support function files>
   ./lib/collections/<collection>/<file>
   ./lib/collections/<collection>/server/<permissions file>

/project_folder/router
   ./client/layouts/<layout file>
   ./lib/<configuration file>
   ./lib/<middleware file>

/project_folder/<module>
   ./<route file>
   ./client/<template file>
```

```
./client/<logic file>
./client/<styles file>
./server/<publishers file>
./server/<methods file>
```

It's important to note that the /lib directory will always run before any other code does. Let's place our canonical file under the /_globals/canonical/server directory.

Let's create our first module: the router. Create the /router/client/layout.jade directory, and we will only have one layout throughout the project. Now let's code our layout:

```
//- LAYOUT.JADE
head
    title Online Shop
    meta(charset="utf-8")

    //- Allow saving to homescreen
    meta(name="apple-mobile-web-app-capable" content="yes")

    //- Do not try to detect phone numbers
    meta(name="format-detection" content="telephone=no")

    //- Make it mobile friendly
    meta(name="viewport" content="user-scalable=no, initial-
    scale=1.0, maximum-scale=1.0")

body

template(name="layout")
    +Template.dynamic(template=nav)
    +Template.dynamic(template=content)
```

Here, we have introduced the Template.dynamic component. This component may be used to render other templates dynamically by changing the value of a variable to the name of the template we want to render. We decided to use two variables—nav and content— that are controlled by the router. So, basically, the content variable will be changing to different strings that are equal to the names of our templates.

We will create our landing module in the next chapter to learn not only how to use the router but also how to properly subscribe to data.

Summary

We have addressed a lot of things in this chapter. We can now program faster because we have tools such as CoffeeScript, Jade, and Stylus to help us. Also, we have learned how to use templates, helpers, and events to work with our Meteor frontend. Understanding the event loop and the merge box has made us a bit more precautious when it comes to running complex, time-consuming operations. Finally, we began to build a project, and we adopted a folder structure that is going to make development quicker.

In the next chapter, we will cover two of the most important parts that make a Meteor application viable: Meteor publishers and Meteor subscribers. With these patterns, you will be able to produce sites that load quickly and that do not put too much strain on the server.

2
Publish and Subscribe Patterns

This is by far the most important chapter in this book. The way we control our publishers and subscribers is going to define how quickly our application responds in production. Publishers and subscribers are the link between our database and the client. The server uses publishers to publish information to the client, while the client requests information from the publishers by subscribing to them. This is all managed via the `Meteor.publish` and `Meteor.subscribe` functions. We should be able to produce the data that the client wants to see with two objectives in mind:

- Reduce stress from the server
- Send only the information that the client needs

This chapter will teach you the different patterns that you can use to attain these objectives for every template that you build. Here is an overview of the topics we will cover to understand these patterns:

- Template-level subscriptions
- Database relationships
- Publishing with relations
- Aggregation publishers
- External API publishers

Template-level subscriptions

This pattern attaches the `Meteor.subscribe` functions to templates. The key advantage of subscribing from the template is the ability to isolate the template and know that it still works when it is rendered.

Many Meteor developers attach their subscription methods to their routes. This means that the template will only render with the correct data at that particular route.

With this pattern, we will be able to reuse templates anywhere without worrying about data.

Setting up products for the online shop

Let's start by setting up a `Products` collection in MongoDB for our `online_shop` project. In *Chapter 1, Getting Started with Meteor* we learned that we need to place this definition under the `/globals/lib/collections` directory:

```
# /globals/lib/collections/products/products.coffee
@Products = new Mongo.Collection "products"

# fields:
#   name
#   description
#   sku
```

It's important to note that we are adding `@` at the beginning of the `Products` variable. This compiles into `this.Products`. In CoffeeScript for Meteor, we do this to define a globally scoped variable. This means that the `Products` variable now exists in every CoffeeScript file that we will create.

We need to add a permission file as well so that we can modify the collection from the console. The `allow`/`deny` functions are rules that add a layer of security to the collections. If an `allow` rule returns `true` for a given action, it will allow the change to pass. For now, we are going to set all the rules to allow everything. We will address permissions when we look at roles in *Chapter 4, Application Patterns*.

```
# /globals
# ./lib/collections/products/server/products_permissions.coffee
Meteor.startup ->
  Products.allow
    insert: -> true
    update: -> true
    remove: -> true
```

We use the `Meteor.startup` function to make sure that we have set up `Products` as a collection before we set the `allow`/`deny` rules. Now that we have a collection, let's make the landing page to show us a list of products. Let's build the **view** first in the `/products/client` directory:

```
//- /products/client/products.jade
template(name="products")
  h3.text-center products
```

This view is just a placeholder. We always need to create the template object before we can actually begin working with the publishers and subscribers.

Building the publisher

Let's construct a simple publisher for our view using the `Meteor.publish` function. This publisher will send only 10 documents to the subscribed clients. We'll discuss pagination in *Chapter 4, Application Patterns*.

```
# /products/server/products_pub.coffee
Meteor.publish "products_pub", ->
  Products.find {},
    limit:10
```

Subscribing to the publisher

This is where the magic begins. We are going to use the `Template.<template>.onCreated` function to subscribe to our publisher. The `onCreated` function runs whenever an instance of the template is created in the DOM. So, if we place a `Meteor.subscribe` function within this function, this will automatically resubscribe whenever the template is used. Let's give it a shot:

```
# /products/client/products.coffee
Template.products.onCreated ->
  @autorun =>
    @subscribe "products_pub"
```

The `this.autorun` function is, basically, a special version of the `Tracker.autorun` function. What does this do? This is meant to rerun whenever its dependencies change. The difference with this special function is that it will automatically stop subscriptions. You'll notice that we are binding `this.autorun` to the context by using `=>`, so we can use the special `this.subscribe` function within the `autorun` block. As expected, the `this.subscribe` functions exactly as `Meteor.subscribe` does. However, it plays a key part in automatically stopping subscriptions as well.

Wait! There's more. This snippet of code can be overwritten by other `onCreated` hooks. This means that if we were to define a second `onCreated` function, the first function will not run. We change this behavior using the `xorax:multiple-callbacks` package. This package, basically, concatenates `onCreated`, `onRendered`, and `onDestroyed` functions so that they cannot be overwritten. Let's take a look:

```coffee
# /products/client/products.coffee
Template.created "products", ->
  @autorun =>
    @subscribe "products_pub"
```

We only need to change the first line of the code. This is done so that we can attach multiple functions to the `onCreated` template hook without overwriting any other functions.

Database relationships

Our collections will always be related in one way or another to other collections in our database. This topic is going to examine the three different types of relationships you should be thinking about when you are designing your database.

The shape that our database will take ultimately defines what our publishers are going to look like. If your data is all mashed up in just one or two different collections, you will very quickly find yourself struggling to filter data. If your data is spread too far between collections, the code will become difficult to maintain in the long run. So what is the solution to this problem?

The solution to database relationships is to understand how the data is going to be used in the client, how often it is going to be modified, and how large the set can be.

Let's build out the rest of our collections to get a notion of what good relationships look like.

One to one

A one to one database relationship describes how one MongoDB document in a collection will be linked to only one other MongoDB document in another collection. You can think of this as a JavaScript object inside another object.

In Meteor, you should create a one to one relationship for a subset of fields that you will use sparingly, that will have unique interfaces, or that you will use without necessarily requiring access to the product. With this relationship, it is going to be very easy to build an image uploader and a collage of images showing only `master_image`.

Start by adding a collection that will handle our products' images: ProductImages. We are going to assume that our frontend is going to have multiple types of images, each one being presented in a different part of the interface that we are building:

```
# /lib/collections/product_images/product_images_collection.coffee
@ProductImages = new Mongo.Collection "product_images"

# fields:
#   product
#   master_image
#   side_image
#   front_image
#   top_image
#   cart_image

# /lib/collections/
# ./product_images/server/product_images_permissions.coffee
Meteor.startup ->
  ProductImages.allow
    insert: -> true
    update: -> true
    remove: -> true
```

The ProductImages collection is going to contain a field named product. This field establishes our relationship by saving the unique _id field from the Products collection. This means that every time we want to publish a product with ProductImages, we need to query the database as well by searching for Product_id within ProductImages. So a helper would look like this:

```
# COFFEESCRIPT
Template.landing.helpers
  "images": ->
    ProductImages.findOne product:@_id
```

One to many

A one to many database relationship describes how one MongoDB document in one collection will be linked to many MongoDB documents in another collection. You can think of this as an array of JavaScript objects that exists under a particular field but the data is so complex that you need to separate it.

Now let's create an `Orders` collection. This collection is going to function as a cart. While your first instinct may be to create a `Carts` collection, you will quickly find that you are duplicating the order information (one for the cart and one for the order, once it is placed). We can easily identify whether an order is new or not by adding a `status` field:

```
# /lib/collections/
# ./orders/orders_collection.coffee
@Orders = new Mongo.Collection "orders"

# fields
  # status ("new","pending","complete")
  # total_products
  # subtotal
  # tax
  #    rate
  #    amount
  # discounts
  #    discount
  #    amount
  # total
  # date_created
```

Let's not forget to add permissions for the collection as well. We need to do this every time we create a new collection to secure the collection from hackers and ensure that the client can modify the collection accordingly. We will cover more on this in the *Security* section of *Chapter 4, Application Patterns*.

```
# /lib/collections/
# ./orders/server/orders_permissions.coffee
Meteor.startup ->
  Orders.allow
    insert: -> true
    update: -> true
    remove: -> true
```

Something is wrong with this, the products are not defined in the collection! We intentionally created an order summary collection that is going to have a one to many relationship with order details. We do not know how extensive the order actually might be. If we include a field that holds an array of products, this list will not only be difficult to manage, but also could potentially become large enough that it will crash the database.

Let's put the details of our order in a separate collection called `OrderDetails`:

```coffee
# /lib/collections/
# ./order_details/order_details_collection.coffee
@OrderDetails = new Mongo.Collection "order_details"

# fields
  # order
  # product
  # price
  # quantity
  # subtotal
  # tax
  #   rate
  #   amount
  # total
  # discounts
  #   discount
  #   amount
```

```coffee
# /lib/collections/
# ./order_details/server/order_details_permissions.coffee
Meteor.startup ->
  OrderDetails.allow
    insert: -> true
    update: -> true
    remove: -> true
```

Perfect! Now we can say one `Order` has many `OrderDetails`. In this scenario, each document in the `OrderDetails` collection represents a single product and the details about that product within the order. We have added the `order` field to identify to which specific order the details (or in this case, the products) belong to.

This is excellent design. By separating the details from the order, we are capable of controlling exactly which data the server sends down to the client. Remember, the goal here is to send the least amount of data possible to the client so that the site loads quickly and stress on the server is reduced. Managing inserts and updates as well becomes easier. As we do not need to deal with indexing a details array, we can simply use IDs to find and manipulate data. Now when the shop admin subscribes to the `Orders` collection, we can do this in such a way that the server only sends the data the admin needs to see the orders. Clicking on an order would then lead to subscribing to only that orders' details.

Many to many

A many to many database relationship describes how many MongoDB documents in one collection will be linked to many MongoDB documents in another collection. You can think of this as a table where you repeat information and only change the information of one field for every row so that you can filter the information by that row.

These types of relationships require a **mapping table**. In the case of MongoDB, a mapping table is a separate collection. A mapping table is the part that repeats information in every row without actually duplicating entries; it simply makes pairs between each collection ID.

In the example that we are going to program, we want to create a many to many relationship between products and tags because a product can have many tags and a tag can have many products. The mapping table in this case is going to save each ID pair. So if a product has two tags, there will be two entries in the mapping table with the same product ID but each with a different tag ID. If a tag is a part of two products, then the mapping table will have two entries with the same tag ID but each one with a different product ID.

It's important to note that these types of relationships are often overlooked because of their complexity. If for some reason you find yourself trying to match two collections with arrays from each collection, you are definitely attempting a "many to many" relationship.

To explain this relationship, we are going to create a `Tags` collection for our products:

```
# /lib/collections/
# ./tags/tags_collection.coffee
@Tags = new Mongo.Collection "tags"

# fields
#   name

# /lib/collections/
# ./tags/server/tags_permissions.coffee
Meteor.startup ->
  Tags.allow
    insert: -> true
    update: -> true
    remove: -> true
```

You will notice that in this type of relationship the `Tags` collection has nothing to associate to a product, but if it did, it would have to be an array of products to which the tag belongs to. To establish the relationship, we will create the mapping table, that is, the `ProductsTags` collection:

```
# /lib/collections/
# ./products_tags/products_tags_collection.coffee
@ProductsTags = new Mongo.Collection "products_tags"

# fields
#   product
#   tag

# /lib/collections/
# ./tags/server/products_tags_permissions.coffee
Meteor.startup ->
  ProductsTags.allow
    insert: -> true
    update: -> true
    remove: -> true
```

This collection allows us to have any combination of relations between `Products` and `Tags`. Suppose we want to see all the products related to one tag. In this case, we will first query the mapping table for that tag and then query the tags using the result.

Beware! Many to many relationships can be difficult to spot. If you are stuck at any point during your database design process, do not forget to consider this possibility.

Publishing with relations

We understand how our collections are related, but how can we make it easy to publish data with these relationships?

In Meteor, it can be problematic to publish relationships because of reactivity and the way publishers work. You would expect that by simply making two queries to two related collections and returning an array will publish a perfectly reactive collection. This is not the case. A `Meteor.publish` function does not rerun when dependencies change. This means that if a relationship is broken, the related document will remain published, or worse if a new relationship is made by another client, the related data will not publish.

To take care of database relationships and reactivity in Meteor, we use the `lepozepo:publish-with-relations` package. This package automatically takes care of subscribing to new data in the most efficient way possible when relationships are broken. If you are familiar with MySQL, this package makes JOINs a breeze.

Publishing products with images (one to one)

We will be working with the `/products` directory, this module will be our landing page. First, let's set up a route for our view:

```
# /products/products_route.coffee
FlowRouter.route "/",
  name:"products"
  action: ->
    FlowLayout.render "layout",
      content:"products"
```

We are using the `FlowRouter.route` function to define the path of our landing page and the `FlowLayout.render` function to define which layout template to use. You will notice that the `FlowLayout.render` function is taking in two parameters: the first one defines which layout template to render, and the second one defines where to render within that layout template.

Now we can work on the publisher. The goal is to publish 10 products paired with only their `master_image`:

```
# /products/server/products_pub.coffee
Meteor.publish "products", ->
  @relations
    collection:Products
    options:
      limit:10
    mappings:[
      {
        key:"product"
        collection:ProductImages
      }
    ]

  @ready()
```

Notice the `mappings` key of the object that we are passing through the `@relations` function. All the objects inside the array must have at least a `collection` key. Optionally, they can take `key` and `foreign_key`. In this case, we use `key` to express that the `_id` field in the `Products` collection is equal to the string of the `product` field in the `ProductImages` collection. This is the most efficient way to publish data. The package will automatically make sure that all changes to the collections are reflected in real time.

The `Meteor.publish` function has one peculiarity: when data changes, the cursor will react accordingly, but the function holding the cursor will not. The impact of this is obvious when it comes to creating relationships. Let's look at what our code would look like without using a package to handle our relationships:

```
# DO NOT CODE THIS INTO YOUR PROJECT
products_cursor = Products.find {},limit:10

# Make products an array with all the _ids
products = products_cursor.map (product) ->
  product._id

# Find their images
images_cursor = ProductImages.find
  product:
    $in:products

# Return the cursors in an array
[products_cursor,images_cursor]
```

In this case, suppose that for some reason the order of the `Products` collection changes. This will make `products_cursor` change reactively as you would expect on the client, but because there were no changes to the `ProductImages` collection and `Meteor.publish` does not rerun when there is a change in one of its dependencies, the images of the newly published products will not be published reactively!

Publishing orders with details (one to many)

Now we will work on our `Orders` and `OrderDetails` collections. Let's set up our template, route, and subscriber for the function that creates orders. We can name this module as `cart` and store it under the `orders` directory:

```
# /orders/cart/client/cart.jade
template(name="cart")
  h3.text-center cart
```

```coffee
# /orders/cart/client/cart.coffee
Template.created "cart", ->
  @autorun =>
    order = Session.get "cart.order"
    @subscribe "cart",
      order:order
```

Notice that the `order` variable is going to get our order `_id` by using the `Session` variables. We do this because the `Session` variables are reactive; if for some reason the value changes, this makes sure that the subscriber reruns. The subscriber reruns because the variable is defined within the `@autorun` function.

Also, we are passing an object as an argument to the `@subscribe` function so that the publisher knows what order we are talking about:

```coffee
# /orders/cart/cart_route.coffee
FlowRouter.route "/cart",
  name:"cart"
  action: ->
    FlowLayout.render "layout",
      content:"cart"
```

We need to publish three different collections to have all the information that our cart needs: `Orders`, `OrderDetails`, and `Products`. This publisher can follow the same logic that we found in the first publisher:

```coffee
# /orders/cart/server/cart_pub.coffee
Meteor.publish "cart", (ops={}) ->
  if ops.order and not _.isEmpty ops.order
    @relations
      collection:Orders
      filter:
        _id:ops.order
        status:"new"
      mappings:[
        {
          key:"order"
          collection:OrderDetails
          options:
            limit:25
          mappings:[
            {
              foreign_key:"product"
              collection:Products
            }
          ]
        }
      ]
```

```
      }
    ]

  @ready()
```

This publisher is predefining defaults for the function by passing `ops={}` within the parameters (another useful shortcut that CoffeeScript provides). After making sure that `ops.order` exists and is not a blank string, we establish our relationships. We need to make sure that the status of `Order` has the `"new"` value for security, so we hardcode it in the `filter` key.

Notice that in this case, we are making use of `foreign_key`. This indicates that the `OrderDetails` collection has a `product` field that contains a string equal to the `_id` field of the `Products` collection.

For now, we are going to limit `OrderDetails` to `25`.

Publishing a tag with products (many to many)

We definitely want to be able to filter our products via tags. We can follow the same pattern from the previous topic. Let's modify our `products` module.

First, our subscriber needs to reactively change to an array of tags _ids. We can use a `Session` variable for now to set an array of tag _ids so that we can easily modify this directly from the console:

```coffee
# /products/client/products.coffee
Template.created "products", ->
  @autorun =>
    # tags is an array of tag _ids
    tags = Session.get "products.tags"
    filter = {}

    if tags and not _.isEmpty tags
      _.extend filter,
        tags:tags

    @subscribe "products", filter
```

We use underscore's `_.extend` function to make sure that the `filter` variable has a `tags` key, if `tags` exist. Now our publisher is going to get a bit more complex:

```coffee
# /products/server/products_pub.coffee
Meteor.publish "products", (ops = {}) ->
  limit = 10

  if ops.tags and not _.isEmpty ops.tags
    @relations
      collection:Tags
      filter:
        _id:
          $in:ops.tags
      mappings:[
        {
          collection:ProductsTags
          key:"tag"
          mappings:[
            {
              collection:Products
              foreign_key:"product"
              options:
                limit:limit
              mappings:[
                {
                  collection:ProductImages
                  key:"product"
                }
              ]
            }
          ]
        }
      ]

  else
    @relations
      collection:Products
      options:
        limit:limit
      mappings:[
        {
          key:"product"
```

```
        collection:ProductImages
    }
  ]
```

```
@ready()
```

While the code may seem long, the logic is easy to understand. First, we filtered our `Tags` collection by using the `tags` array that we had defined in our subscriber. Then we chained the relations using a combination of `key` and `foreign_key`. The function that the mapping table (`ProductsTags`) serves is clear in this scenario.

Key, foreign key, options, and filter

The core concepts to understand from the `lepozepo:publish-with-relations` package are simply the options provided within the `@relations` function.

Both `key` and `foreign_key` default to the `_id` field. The `key` always makes reference to a field within the collection while the `foreign_key` always makes reference to a field of the parent collection.

The `options` and `filter` options are equivalent to the second and first arguments (respectively) of a Meteor - MongoDB query: `Products.find(filter, options)`.

There are many packages that work similar to `lepozepo:publish-with-relations`, and we are not exploring them in this book, but they are certainly worth keeping an eye on: `reywood:publish-composite`, `lepozepo:reactive-publish`, and `cottz:publish-relations`. I have found the last package to be the best of the bunch because it is simple to use and forces the developer to create smarter database relationships.

Aggregation publishers

Sometimes our database has a considerable amount of information that we want to synthesize. Some developers choose to publish all the information to the client and have the client synthesize it. This, as we have learned so far, can have a negative impact on performance. Other developers might use `Meteor.method` to return the synthesized data. This is definitely better for the client, but it will take a toll on our server if the computation is large.

The best way to handle a problem like this is to use MongoDB's aggregation framework to take the hard work of the calculation to our database, and then we can pair the results with the `Meteor.publish` special functions: `@added`, `@changed`, and `@removed`.

The aggregation framework

MongoDB's aggregation framework uses the concept of a pipeline to process data. A pipeline is, basically, a series of steps that Mongo is going to follow to produce the data you need.

We have installed support for the aggregation framework by adding `meteorhacks:aggregate`. This gives us access to all of the framework's server-side commands. The most common commands that you will end up using are `$match`, `$group`, and `$project`.

Let's build a publisher for our `dashboard` module and start by building the template:

```
# /dashboard/client/dashboard.jade
template(name="dashboard")
  h3.text-center dashboard


# /dashboard/client/dashboard.coffee
Template.created "dashboard", ->
  @autorun =>
    @subscribe "dashboard"


# /dashboard/dashboard_route.coffee
FlowRouter.route "/dashboard",
  name:"dashboard"
  action: ->
    FlowLayout.render "layout",
      content:"dashboard"
```

Now we need to build a collection that exists only on the client. Our server will communicate with this collection manually. We specifically place this collection on the client side because we do not want the server to record data onto the database. We can append the collection to the (`/dashboard/client/dashboard.coffee`) client controller file:

```
# /dashboard/client/dashboard.coffee
@_dashboard = new Mongo.Collection "_dashboard"

Template.created "dashboard", ->
  @autorun =>
    @subscribe "dashboard"
```

As this collection is client-side, we have differentiated it with an underscore at the beginning of the name. This, of course, is not required, but it helps prevent duplicate collection names.

Our goal is to publish the sum of the total and subtotal for the `"pending"` orders. The steps for our pipeline are simple:

1. Filter the collection to show orders with status equal to `"pending"`.

2. Sum the totals of every filtered order:

```
# /dashboard/server/dashboard_pub.coffee
Meteor.publish "dashboard", ->
  totals = Orders.aggregate [
    {
      $match:
        status:"pending"
    }
    {
      $group:
        _id:null
        total:
          $sum:"$total"
        subtotal:
          $sum:"$subtotal"
        discount:
          $sum:"$discount.amount"
    }
  ]

  console.log totals
```

To use the aggregation framework, you use the `.aggregate` function that is attached to the collection object; `Orders`, in this case. This function only takes an array as a parameter—this is because the array is the ordered set of steps that the framework is going to follow. Each step is represented by an object within the array and always begins with an operator.

Here we have decided to use `$match` to filter the orders to find the pending orders, and then we have used `$group` to accumulate the values of `total` and `subtotal`. Notice that the `$group` expression has a mandatory `_id` key. This key defines how we want to group the collection. By setting the `_id` key to `null`, we are stating that we want all the documents in the collection grouped into one single object.

`$sum` is an accumulator operator. When you use an operator like this, you can access a document property by using the money sign ($) followed by the name of the field within a string. Also, you can access objects within objects using the dot notation (`"$discount.amount"`).

The result of `totals` is an array containing a single object with the keys: `total`, `subtotal`, and `discount`.

Publishing the results

Publishing the results is much easier than it seems. We only need to use the `@added` function that is bound to `Meteor.publish`. The `@added` function, basically, informs the subscriber that data has been added to the published set:

```
# /dashboard/server/dashboard_pub.coffee
Meteor.publish "dashboard", ->
  totals = Orders.aggregate [
    {
      $match:
        status:"pending"
    }
    {
      $group:
        _id:null
        total:
          $sum:"$total"
        subtotal:
          $sum:"$subtotal"
        discount:
          $sum:"$discount.amount"
    }
  ]

  if totals and totals.length > 0 and totals[0]
    @added "_dashboard","totals",totals[0]
```

The last two lines make sure that the `totals` array exists, and if it does not, then we publish the first object within the array to our `_dashboard` collection. The `@added` function has three required parameters. The first parameter is the name of the collection, the second is the `_id` of the document, and the third is the document.

Notice that these kinds of publishers are not reactive, which means that we do not need to add a `@changed` or `@removed` function. We can take this a step further though. Instead of creating a collection for every module that needs an aggregation publisher, we can create one master collection that manages all our aggregation publishers.

First, we remove our `_dashboard` collection and create a new `Aggregate` collection:

```
# /dashboard/client/dashboard.coffee
Template.created "dashboard", ->
  @autorun =>
    @subscribe "dashboard"
```

```
# /globals/lib/collections/aggregate/client/aggregate.coffee
@Aggregate = new Mongo.Collection "aggregate"
```

Now, we need to modify our publisher:

```
# /dashboard/server/dashboard_pub.coffee
Meteor.publish "dashboard", ->
  totals = Orders.aggregate [
      {
        $match:
          status:"pending"
      }
      {
        $group:
          _id:null
          total:
            $sum:"$total"
          subtotal:
            $sum:"$subtotal"
          discount:
            $sum:"$discount.amount"
      }
    ]

  if totals and totals.length > 0 and totals[0]
    @added "aggregate","dashboard.totals",totals[0]
```

With this, we can now access our values by calling the following function on our client-side console:

```
Aggregate.findOne "dashboard.totals"
```

It's important to understand that as soon as we leave the route, the subscriber will be stopped and the `aggregate` collection will be cleared. This default behavior gives this collection a lot of flexibility.

Why is using the aggregation framework with a publisher more effective than with `Meteor.method`? The Meteor methods are designed to trigger critical functions within our server and respond with a simple message. On the other hand, publishers are designed to control data sets. You will very quickly find that publishers are easier to control and optimize than methods.

External API publishers

These types of publishers should be avoided. They are great to get raw data from external services such as **Stripe** or **Square**, but they tend to be little bit slower because this involves actively communicating with another server. When we are integrating with other servers, we should always build a separate synchronization server. We will talk about APIs in another chapter.

Still, this publishing pattern can be useful in edge cases, so it is important to know that this option exists.

The HTTP package

HTTP is a protocol for collaborative systems; it is the protocol that allows users to connect to web pages. The HTTP protocol can be used to access data from other servers from our own server.

We are going to use Meteor's integrated HTTP `Request` module to communicate with Stripe's servers. We chose to integrate with Stripe because it is a payment processor that is easy to integrate and more reliable than most other payment processors in the market. We have added this package when we ran `meteor add http`. This module has all the functions that you would expect: `.get`, `.post`, `.put`, and `.del`. For this topic, we are only going to cover the `.get` function.

Our goal is to get data from Stripe. Start by creating a free account in Stripe. After you have created your account, go to your dashboard and set it to `"test"`.

Now create a payment by clicking on **+ Create Payment**. Use the following data for the payment:

- **Amount**: `10`
- **Card Number**: `4242 4242 4242 4242`

In our test environment, we do not need to add CVC, and Stripe automatically sets the expiration date to a year from today.

Click on **Account Settings** and copy your test secret key. We are going to use this to authorize our request.

We can start by creating a new publisher under `/dashboard_pub.coffee`; we are only going to get the last three charges — we will modify this later:

```
# /dashboard/server/dashboard_pub.coffee
Meteor.publish "dashboard", ->
    ...
```

```
Meteor.publish "latest_sales", ->
  @unblock()

  HTTP.get "https://api.stripe.com/v1/charges?limit=3",
    headers:
      "Authorization":"Bearer <TEST SECRET KEY>"
    (error,result) =>
      if not error
        _.each result.data.data, (payment) =>
          @added "aggregate",
          "dashboard.sales.#{Meteor.uuid()}",payment
      else
        console.log error
```

The `@unblock` function that we are using here has been made available via the `meteorhacks:unblock` package. It works the same way as the `@unblock` function does in `Meteor.methods`; this makes sure that the publisher does not block the server while it is waiting for information from Stripe to arrive. Unblocking the aggregation publishers is crucial! If we do not unblock the publisher, then we risk the client becoming unresponsive when the user navigates away from the page.

You might be asking yourself: can't we just make the HTTP request on the client and not worry about blocking the server? No, we cannot. If you were to run this function on the client, you would have to expose your secret key, and this is a major security flaw.

The `HTTP.get` function has three important fields: the URL, the `options` object, and the callback function. The URL is the address that Stripe provides in their API documentation—in this case, we have used the `/charges` URL and passed a parameter `limit` to get the last three sales. The options object is used to pass all the information that the request needs. In this case, we will use the `headers` key to set our `Authorization` header. There are several keys that the options object can take; you can find these at `docs.meteor.com`. Our callback function receives the result from the request. As with most functions in Meteor, it returns two arguments; the first one is an error object that is undefined if there is no error, while the second one is the actual result.

In this case, the data that we are looking for is contained within `result.data.data` as an array. We can then easily publish the data with our `@added` function. Notice that we are binding both the callback and the `_.each` function, so we can have access to `@added`.

Let's subscribe to our new publisher to see our data:

```coffee
# /dashboard/client/dashboard.coffee
Template.created "dashboard", ->
  @autorun =>
    @subscribe "dashboard"
    @subscribe "latest_sales"
```

Try running `Aggregate.find().fetch()` in your console to see the results.

Summary

In this chapter, we learned how to isolate subscribers from templates using template hooks. Also, we learned how to optimize the structure of our database depending on how we are going to use it. When it comes to publishers, we learned how to return every possible data structure without breaking reactivity. We covered aggregation publishers and learned how to synthesize data before we publish it, without hurting the performance of the server.

In the next chapter, we will cover a handful of frontend techniques that will help us to keep our code flexible and our frontend looking great.

3
Front-end Patterns

This chapter will cover a useful set of patterns that will speed up your frontend workflow. Meteor makes it easy to build rich frontend experiences, but we have to be careful with the number of computations our interface requires to function. Too many computations will slow down mobile devices. In this chapter, we are going to learn how to keep our computations short, DOM simple, and animations effective. You will learn the following topics:

- Responsive design
- Super helpers
- Variable types
- Quick forms
- Loading
- Animations
- Search engine optimization

Responsive design

An application is always judged by how it looks. Now that we know how to make it perform, we need to learn how to make it look good. Nowadays, it is common practice to build the frontend while keeping the following two things in mind:

- **Minimalism**: This style of design makes your site concise by exposing only the necessary elements to have the site functioning. Less is more.
- **Responsive**: This style of programming makes your site usable everywhere, no matter how big the screen is. The HTML markup will always adapt depending on the width of the screen.

Here, we are only going to cover how to program a responsive frontend because minimalism is a vast and highly debatable topic.

General settings

The first layer of customization begins with the `kyleking:customizable-bootstrap-stylus` package that we have already installed. Follow these steps to set this up:

Create the following directory:

`/_globals/client/bootstrap/custom.bootstrap.json`.

(Leave the JSON file empty.)

Run the Meteor project using this:

meteor

You will notice three new files have been added. These files will compile at runtime to produce your version of Twitter Bootstrap.

Open `/_globals/client/bootstrap/custom.bootstrap.json`, and make sure that all variables are set to `true`:

```
{"_route":"/_globals/client/bootstrap/custom.bootstrap.json"},
{
  "modules" : {
    "variables": true,
    "mixins": true,

    "normalize": true,
    "print": true,
    "glyphicons": true,

    "scaffolding": true,
    "utilities": true,
    "type": true,
    "code": true,
    "grid": true,
    "tables": true,
    "forms": true,
    "buttons": true,

    "component-animations": true,
    "dropdowns": true,
    "button-groups": true,
```

```
                    "input-groups": true,
                    "navs": true,
                    "navbar": true,
                    "breadcrumbs": true,
                    "pagination": true,
                    "pager": true,
                    "labels": true,
                    "badges": true,
                    "jumbotron": true,
                    "thumbnails": true,
                    "alerts": true,
                    "progress-bars": true,
                    "media": true,
                    "list-group": true,
                    "panels": true,
                    "responsive-embed": true,
                    "wells": true,
                    "close": true,

                    "modals": true,
                    "tooltip": true,
                    "popovers": true,
                    "carousel": true,

                    "responsive-utilities": true
                }
            }
```

By setting all the variables to `true`, we are reeling in all the functionality that `bootstrap` has. If there is anything you do not want to use from the framework, you can deactivate it by setting it to `false` in this file.

You will need to manually restart Meteor for these changes to take effect. So press *Ctrl* + *C* on your terminal to stop Meteor and run the `meteor` command again.

Now we can edit `bootstrap`. Start by opening the `/_globals/client/bootstrap/custom.bootstrap.import.styl` directory. Here, you are going to find a library of the Stylus variables that we can play with.

Let's remove rounded corners and modify button border colors:

```
// /_globals/client/bootstrap/custom.bootstrap.import.styl

...

// Line #114
$border-radius-base ?=        0px
$border-radius-large ?=       0px
$border-radius-small ?=       0px
```

. . .

```
// Line #156
$btn-default-color ?=              #333
$btn-default-bg ?=                 #fff
$btn-default-border ?=            $btn-default-color

$btn-primary-color ?=             #fff
$btn-primary-bg ?=                $brand-primary
$btn-primary-border ?=            $btn-primary-bg

$btn-success-color ?=             #fff
$btn-success-bg ?=                $brand-success
$btn-success-border ?=           $btn-success-bg

$btn-info-color ?=                #fff
$btn-info-bg ?=                   $brand-info
$btn-info-border ?=              $btn-info-bg

$btn-warning-color ?=             #fff
$btn-warning-bg ?=               $brand-warning
$btn-warning-border ?=           $btn-warning-bg

$btn-danger-color ?=              #fff
$btn-danger-bg ?=                $brand-danger
$btn-danger-border ?=           $btn-danger-bg
```

What if we need to use bootstrap mixins and variables for custom style sheets? We can use the @import command whenever we need to gain access to everything:

```
@import "_globals/bootstrap/client/custom.bootstrap.import.styl"
```

Let's customize our products page by adding a large promoter. Rewrite the products template with a new #promoter header:

//- /products/client/products.jade

```
template(name="products")
  div#products.template
    header#promoter
      h3 Your Brand
```

Before we write our product styles, let's create a global style sheet for any application-wide styling at /_globals/client/main.styl. Here, we are going to make sure that our initial views are set correctly so that we may properly make use of relative units:

// /_globals/client/main.styl

```
html, body, #__flow-root, #__flow-root > .template
```

```
html, body, body > .template
    height:100%
```

With this set of rules, we are basically making sure that everything has the height of the viewport including our first `.template` DOM element. This technique allows us to have relative percentage heights work as expected.

We also need to set the root DOM element for BlazeLayout. Let's do this in a client/server configuration file:

```
# /_globals/router/config.coffee

if Meteor.isClient
  BlazeLayout.setRoot 'body'
```

Now, create the directory for the `products` styles: /products/client/products.`styl`. We will start by importing our variables into the file and setting some simple rules to make the promoter look good:

```
// products/client/products.styl
@import "_globals/bootstrap/custom.bootstrap.import.styl"

#products
  #promoter
    background: $brand-primary
    height: 80%
```

Great, this sets up our `promoter` section for any promotional images that we may want to add, and the site looks decent (but not good enough yet) on mobile.

Bootstrap

Bootstrap is a library of CSS rules that makes development of simple layouts quick, thanks to the library of classes that it includes.

Let's extend our products template to upgrade our `#promoter` header and add a `#features` section. We will use bootstrap to manage the grid in this case:

```
//- /products/client/products.jade

template(name="products")
  div#products.template
    header#promoter
      div.container
        div.row
```

```
          div.col-xs-12
            h3 Your Brand

      section#features
        div.container
          div.row
            div.col-xs-12.col-sm-4
              h3.text-center
                span.fa-stack.fa-lg
                  i.fa.fa-square.fa-stack-2x.text-primary
                  i.fa.fa-users.fa-inverse.fa-stack-1x
              h5.text-center 24 Hour Support

            div.col-xs-12.col-sm-4
              h3.text-center
                span.fa-stack.fa-lg
                  i.fa.fa-square.fa-stack-2x.text-primary
                  i.fa.fa-truck.fa-inverse.fa-stack-1x
              h5.text-center Next Day Delivery

            div.col-xs-12.col-sm-4
              h3.text-center
                span.fa-stack.fa-lg
                  i.fa.fa-square.fa-stack-2x.text-primary
                  i.fa.fa-bomb.fa-inverse.fa-stack-1x
              h5.text-center Mind Blown Guarantee
```

We are doing quite a few things here but nothing complex. First, we wrapped the contents of our #promoter header in bootstraps' grid. Bootstrap grids work only as advertised when they are under a row class. The container class controls our page-wide breakpoints.

Bootstrap columns are set using the col- class prefix followed by the target screen size, then an optional offset indicator, and finally, the number of columns that the element will span or offset:

```
div.col-<screen size>-<optional offset>-<number of columns>
```

Class	Breakpoint	Offset
col-xs-*	<768px	col-xs-offset-*
col-sm-*	≥768px	col-sm-offset-*
col-md-*	≥992px	col-md-offset-*
col-lg-*	≥1200px	col-lg-offset-*

Bootstrap has a total of 12 columns (this can be modified in our `variables` file); each column supports offsetting and nesting too. Remember, the smallest screen size will override all other screen sizes if the other screen sizes are not defined. So, if you want three columns of every size, you will only need to define it for the smallest size screen. In this example, we are separating our `#features` section into three columns of every size above 768 px and treating this as a single column in anything below 768 px.

If at any point you need to nest bootstrap columns, then you will need to place these new columns under a `row` class. The following example centers a six-column long `div` inside another six-column long `div`:

```
div.row
  div.col-xs-6
  div.col-xs-6
    div.row
      div.col-xs-6.col-xs-offset-3
```

We are using Font Awesome to create some icons for our `#features` section as well. Here, we are using one of the Font Awesome's lesser known **icon stacking** feature. To use this feature, you only need to wrap a set of Font Awesome icons with a `span.fa-stack` element.

Font Awesome has a list of about 500 icons. If you want to use a different set of icons, feel free to check out the list of icons online at `http://fortawesome.github.io/Font-Awesome/icons`.

Now let's add a little bit of Jeet and Rupture to our frontend.

Jeet grid systems with Rupture

The version of Stylus that we have installed (`mquandalle:stylus`) comes packaged with a lot of useful mixins, the most notable ones being **Jeet** and **Rupture**. Jeet is a grid system that is superior to Twitter Bootstrap because it is more flexible, and Rupture is a set of functions that simplifies media queries. Knowing how to leverage both Jeet and Twitter Bootstrap will increase the quality of your frontend designs.

Let's patch up our `#promoter` header to make our page more user friendly for users that are in landscape mode on smaller devices:

```
// products/client/products.styl
@import "_globals/client/bootstrap/custom.bootstrap.import.styl"
@import "jeet" // Add jeet
```

```
#products
  #promoter
    background: $brand-primary
    height: 80%

    +below($screen-sm-min) // If the screen width is smaller than
    -sm
      +portrait() // And the device is in portrait mode
        height: 30%

      +landscape() // And the device is in landscape mode
        col(1/3)
        height: 100%

  #features
    +below($screen-sm-min) // If the screen width is smaller than
    -sm
      +landscape() // And the device is in landscape mode
        col(2/3)
        height: 100%

        .container
          width:100% // Override bootstrap container
```

Rupture adds several mixins to easily control the @media queries: below, above, between, landscape, portrait and many more. You will find yourself using below, landscape, and portrait more often than the rest. To use these mixins in Stylus, we simply prefix a plus sign (+) before the command.

In this example, we are using +below($screen-sm-min) to define the CSS rules for all the devices whose widths are below bootstrap's -sm breakpoint. Then we will use +portrait() and +landscape() to define CSS rules for portrait and landscape modes.

Next, we will use Jeet to control master columns using the col() mixin. This mixin takes in a fraction that defines the width of the element as a fraction. Consider the numerator as the number of columns that you want the element to take up and the denominator as the total number of columns:

```
col(<column width>/<number of columns>)
```

In this example, when we switch to landscape mode on a small device, our #promoter header is one column wide out of three, while our #features section is two columns wide out of three.

Super helpers

In Meteor, you will quickly find yourself repeating helpers among templates for simple things such as formatting. We can prevent repetition by creating a global dictionary of functions—this is what we call a super helper. To do this, we are going to tap into Meteor's rendering engine—Blaze.

It is important to understand that Blaze is deeply integrated with Spacebars, and Spacebars is Meteor's updated version of HandlebarsJS. HandlebarsJS is a JavaScript templating engine that enables the use of helpers and components on the frontend using {{}}. This legacy means that Spacebars has a lot of the HandlebarsJS functionality. So, much of the documentation found in HandlebarsJS applies to Meteor helpers as well.

Defining a Blaze helper

Meteor exposes the `Template.registerHelper` function to create global helpers. Let's create something to help us format money:

```coffee
# /_globals/client/formatters.coffee

Template.registerHelper "format_money", (value) ->
  if _.isNumber value
    "$#{(value / 100).toFixed(2)}"
```

As you can see, the syntax for a global helper is exactly the same as it would be for a template helper. Now, we can use this helper in any template. Let's create a product template under our /products directory for our `products` template and try it out here:

```jade
//- /products/client/product.jade

template(name="product")
  div.col-xs-12.col-sm-4.col-md-3
    article#product
      h5 {{name}}

      div.offer
        span.price {{format_money price}}
```

We will need to patch our products template as well:

```jade
//- /products/client/products.jade

template(name="products")
```

```
div#products.template
  header#promoter
    ...
  section#features
    ...

  br
  section#featured_products
    div.container
      div.row
        each products
          +product
```

Let's add some temporary entries to our products collection. We will use these entries throughout the rest of the chapter:

```
@Products = new Mongo.Collection "products"

if Meteor.isServer
  if Products.find().count() is 0
    Products.insert
      name:"Nuka Cola"
      price: 1099

    Products.insert
      name:"1up Soda"
      price: 999

    Products.insert
      name:"JuggerNog"
      price: 899


# /products/client/products.coffee

Template.created "products", ->
  ...

Template.products.helpers
  products: ->
    Products.find()
```

Note that in this data schema we are defining `price` in cents. This is a common practice when dealing with money in JavaScript to avoid arithmetic floating point issues. What does this mean? Go to your web browser's console, and run the following operation: `0.1 + 0.2`. Oddly enough, JavaScript does not respond with `0.3`; it responds with `0.3000000000004` instead. The reason for this is JavaScript's internal 64-bit floating point representation of decimal numbers. This means that JavaScript does not fully understand what a decimal number is. This is why, we do not use decimal numbers when we deal with money, we just use the smallest available denomination.

Making a global dictionary

Wait, we can still make this formatter more widely available in our application. Let's turn this into a dictionary and share it with our controllers. In other words, we want to be able to use a helper such as `{{format.money amount}}` and use this in our CoffeeScript in the form of `format.money amount` as well:

```
# /_globals/client/formatters.coffee

@format =
  money: (value) ->
    if _.isNumber value
      "$#{(value / 100).toFixed(2)}"

Template.registerHelper "format", ->
  format
```

First, we create an object that holds our definitions, and we make it global using `@` (which is equal to `this`). Then we place this object of definitions inside a global helper. Simple! Now we know how to build a super helper that we can use anywhere. To test this, type `format.money(1099)` in your browser's console; this should return **"$10.99"**.

Variable types

There are four types of variables that we need to understand to optimize our frontend workflow: **session**, **persistent**, **file scope**, and **ReactiveVar**. With these variables, we can build dynamic sites easily based on how the user is interacting with the view.

The session variables are variables that exist only during a session. A session begins whenever a user hits the site. These variables can be shared across routes and are reactive.

The persistent variables are variables that are stored in local storage so that they can be read even after the session closes.

The file scoped variables are variables that only exist within the scope of the file. These are generally not reactive.

The ReactiveVar variables can be scoped to the file or globally and are reactive. These variables do not persist the way session variables do.

Session variables

Some Meteor developers believe that session variables are overused. This is definitely true, if you are not managing them. For the most part, session variables should be used to handle data that is shared across multiple routes in your application, have no place in your database, need reactivity, and persist through a hot code reload.

If you stop and think about it, not many things require all of these attributes. At first, you may rely on them heavily to control your frontend, but as your frontend becomes more minimal, you will realize there is no need for them.

Still, if you are going to use them, you should follow two rules to maintain them, as shown here:

- Template-based taxonomy
- Clear them if you are not going to use them

The taxonomy of session variables should always follow the `<template.variable>` pattern to keep them from polluting each other. Suppose we want to control a global alert using session variables, the session variable would look like this:

```
Session.set "products.alert",true
```

Once our user leaves the view, we should clear the session variable. The `clear` function is added by the `u2622:persistent-session` package that we installed in *Chapter 1, Getting Started with Meteor*:

```
# Clear "products.alert" variable after "products" template is
destroyed
Template.destroyed "products", ->
  Session.clear "products.alert"


# Clear all variables after the "products" template is destroyed
Template.destroyed "products", ->
  Session.clear()
```

Do not use session variables along with Meteor methods to obtain server data. While the method works, it makes your data vulnerable and easy to modify on the client.

Also, try to stay away from using session variables that are composed of complex objects with multiple keys or arrays. You will quickly find yourself using lesser lookup tools such as `_.find` and `_.findWhere` to use the data.

Persistent variables

Persistent variables are session variables that persist through a session. In Meteor, a common session variable will reset if the user refreshes the page. Persistent variables leverage AmplifyJS, which in turn uses HTML5 local storage and fallbacks to store the variable inside the user's browser. These types of variables exist because of the `u2622:persistent-session` package.

We can use this variable to keep track of our users' orders, in case they leave the site and are not logged in. So, if the user opens up an order and fills it with items, they can come back to it later without making a user account on our site.

Let's create an `add-to-cart` button that will leverage the persistent variables:

```coffee
# /products/client/product.coffee

Template.product.events
  "click button.add-to-cart": (event) ->
    # Get the session variable
    order_id = Session.get "global.order"
    order = Orders.findOne order_id

    # Insert Order if it doesn't exist
    unless order
      order_id = Orders.insert
        status:"new"
        total_products:0
        subtotal:0
        total:0
    else
      order_id = order._id

    # Set the session variable for future reference
    Session.setPersistent "global.order",order_id
```

```coffee
# Find the order
order = Orders.findOne order_id

# Check for details on this product
detail = OrderDetails.findOne
  product:@_id
  order:order._id

if detail
  # Increase by one if the details exist
  OrderDetails.update detail._id,
    $inc:
      quantity:1

  Orders.update order._id,
    $inc:
      total_products:1
      subtotal:@price
      total:@price
else
  # Insert if details do not exist
  OrderDetails.insert
    quantity:1
    product:@_id
    order:order._id

  Orders.update order._id,
    $inc:
      total_products:1
      subtotal:@price
      total:@price
```

We will need to build a publisher for this to work, but we have to make a choice. As we have both `products` and `product` template, each one could subscribe to a publisher and pull in the same data. Should we subscribe from the `product` or the `products` template? Let's do both! Extending the products publisher will ensure that we get all the data that the template needs while the attached publisher will help us manage our "product details" page and promos when we need it to:

```coffee
# /products/server/products_pub.coffee
Meteor.publish "products", (ops={}) ->
  ...

  if ops.order and not _.isEmpty ops.order
    @relations
```

```
collection:Orders
filter:
  _id:ops.order
  status:"new"
mappings:[
  {
    collection:OrderDetails
    key:"order"
  }
]
```

Then we wire up our subscriber with the order key on the client side:

```
# /products/client/products.coffee

Template.created "products", ->
  @autorun =>
    ...

    order = Session.get "global.order"
    if order and not _.isEmpty order
      _.extend filter,
        order:order

    @subscribe "products", filter
```

With this, now we can add products to an order, refresh the site, and still come back to our order. Let's finish building the publisher for the `product` template:

```
# /products/server/product_pub.coffee

Meteor.publish "product", (ops={}) ->
  if ops.product and not _.isEmpty ops.product
    @relations
      collection:Products
      options:
        _id:ops.product
      mappings:[
        {
          key:"product"
          collection:ProductImages
        }
        {
          collection:ProductsTags
          key:"product"
```

```
          mappings: [
            {
              collection:Tags
              foreign_key:"tag"
            }
          ]
        }
      ]


      if ops.order and not _.isEmpty ops.order
        @relations
          collection:Orders
          filter:
            _id:ops.order
            status:"new"
          mappings:[
            {
              collection:OrderDetails
              key:"order"
              filter:
                product:ops.product
            }
          ]


    @ready()
```

Notice that our product is bringing in only the data that is pertinent to that product and for that order. Now we can program our subscriber:

 # /products/client/product.coffee

```
Template.created "product", ->
  @autorun =>
    filter = {}

    # Get the product ID from the context
    product = @data._id
    _.extend filter,
      product:product

    # Get the order if any
    order = Session.get "global.order"
    if order and not _.isEmpty order
```

```
    _.extend filter,
      order:order


  @subscribe "product", filter

...
```

File scope variables

These are the types of variables you will want to use most of the time. What are they? They are regular variables! This means that they are not reactive, so watch out. Regular variables are scoped for the file only, so you do not need to worry about interfering with the variables that are named the same in other files.

These variables are useful for things such as lists that you know will not change and that you will not need anywhere else in the application. To use one, simply type out a variable outside your Meteor-specific functions.

The ReactiveVar variables

The ReactiveVar variables are reactive variables that are not available to the console in the way that session variables are. This makes them great for things that are reactive and that we want to keep relatively difficult to access for the user from the console.

If at any point you are creating a highly reactive interface, you should fill it up with these variables so that you do not have to worry about managing them. These variables cleared automatically if there is a hot code reload or a page refresh.

To create a reactive variable, you simply define a variable with its constructor:

```
reactive_variable = new ReactiveVar(<optional-default-value>)
```

This variable will expose setter and getter functions. This means that you use the .get command to see the value of the variable and the .set command to change it:

```
# Get the value of the variable
reactive_variable.get()

# Set the value of the variable
reactive_variable.set "hello"
```

Let's use the ReactiveVar variables to create a rich number input interface for our quantity field. We will start by defining a route name as `order_quantity` with a `product` parameter:

```coffee
# /orders/cart/cart_route.coffee

FlowRouter.route "/cart",
  ...

FlowRouter.route "/cart/:product/quantity",
  name:"order_quantity"
  action: ->
    FlowLayout.render "layout",
      content:"order_quantity"
```

We can wire up our product with a new button that will take us to the modify quantity view and passes to our product ID:

```coffee
# /products/client/product.coffee

Template.created "product", ->
  ...

Template.product.events
  "click button.add-to-cart": (event) ->
    ...

  "click button.modify-quantity": ->
    FlowRouter.go "order_quantity",
      product:@_id
```

```jade
//- /products/client/product.jade

template(name="product")
  div.col-xs-12.col-sm-4.col-md-3
    article#product
      h5 {{name}}

      div.offer
        span.price {{format.money price}}

      button.add-to-cart.btn.btn-block.btn-primary Add to Cart

      button.modify-quantity.btn.btn-block.btn-info Quantity
```

Now we need to design a responsive number pad. First, let's add a global `vertical-align` class to our `/_globals/client/main.styl` directory so that we can easily align things vertically:

```
// /_globals/client/main.styl

.vertical-align
  position:relative
  transform:translateY(-50%)
  top:50%
```

We will use Jeet to control this design since it requires more specific control of our DOM elements. Let's start by creating the layout of the page in our `order_quantity` template:

```
//- /orders/cart/client/order_quantity.jade

template(name="order_quantity")
  div#order_quantity.template
    section#number
      h1.text-center.vertical-align {{total}}

    section#number-pad
      each numbers
        div.number
          h2.text-center.vertical-align {{number}}

      div.delete
        p.text-center.vertical-align
          i.fa.fa-undo.fa-2x

      div.add-to-cart
        p.text-center.vertical-align
          i.fa.fa-check.fa-2x
```

Notice that we are using the `vertical-align` class on the element that we want to align vertically. We are going to make each of these elements a large button. Also, we will create a `numbers` helper to write out our numbers to the number pad, and the `total` helper will be our reactive variable. Let's have a look at our styles before we create our helpers:

```
// /orders/cart/client/order_quantity.styl

@import "_globals/client/bootstrap/custom.bootstrap.import.styl"
@import "jeet" // Add jeet
```

```
#order_quantity
  overflow:hidden
  background:$brand-primary
  color:white

  section#number
    height:50%
    h1
      margin:0

  section#number-pad
    height:50%
    .number, .delete, .add-to-cart
      cursor:pointer
      height:25%
      col(1/3,gutter:0,cycle:3)
      h2, p
        margin:0
```

In this example, we have passed the parameters to Jeet: `gutter` and `cycle`. Gutter makes sure that there are no margins, while cycle makes sure that the elements can only make rows with a maximum of 3 elements per row. We have made each section take up exactly 50 percent of the height of the screen but ensured that scrolling wouldn't happen by setting `overflow` to hidden. Knowing that we are always going to have four rows of numbers, we set our height for each number to 25 percent.

Now let's put our `ReactiveVar` variable knowledge to work. First, we set up our variable and attach it to the template instance using this:

```
# /orders/cart/client/order_quantity.coffee


# Attach a reactive variable to the instance
# this variable controls our total
Template.created "order_quantity", ->
  @total = new ReactiveVar()
```

Let's build the `numbers` helper and the helper that will render our (`total`) reactive variable:

```
# /orders/cart/client/order_quantity.coffee


...


Template.order_quantity.helpers
  # Create a list of numbers for the number pad
```

```coffee
"numbers": ->
  _.map [1,2,3,4,5,6,7,8,9,0], (v,k) ->
    number:String v


# Get the reactive variable
# this will automatically update when the variable changes
"total": ->
  Template.instance().total.get()
```

We need to handle the events to update our `ReactiveVar` variable:

```coffee
# /orders/cart/client/order_quantity.coffee


...


Template.order_quantity.events
  # Concatenate numbers to make it work like a number pad
  "click .number": (event,i) ->
    total = i.total.get()

    if total
      new_total = "#{total}#{@number}"
    else
      new_total = "#{@number}"

    i.total.set new_total


  # Remove last number from string
  "click .delete": (event,i) ->
    total = i.total.get()

    if total
      i.total.set total.slice 0,-1

  "click .add-to-cart": (event,i) ->
    # Get the session variable
    order_id = Session.get "global.order"
    order = Orders.findOne order_id

    # Get the total
    total = i.total.get()
    unless total
      return
    else
```

```
total = Number total

# Get the product with the ID from the router
product = Products.findOne FlowRouter.current().params.product

# Insert Order if it doesn't exist
unless order
  order_id = Orders.insert
    status:"new"
    total_products:0
    subtotal:0
    total:0
else
  order_id = order._id

# Set the session variable for future reference
Session.setPersistent "global.order",order_id

# Find the order
order = Orders.findOne order_id

# Check for details on this product
detail = OrderDetails.findOne
  product:product._id
  order:order._id

if detail
  # Increase by one if the details exist
  OrderDetails.update detail._id,
    $inc:
      quantity:total

  Orders.update order_id,
    $inc:
      total_products:1
      subtotal:product.price * total
      total:product.price * total
else
  # Insert if details do not exist
  OrderDetails.insert
    quantity:total
    product:product
    order:order._id
```

```
Orders.update order._id,
  $inc:
    total_products:1
    subtotal:product.price * total
    total:product.price * total


FlowRouter.go "products"
```

If you take a good look at how the add-to-cart event works, you will notice that it is almost identical to the event that we wrote for the products template. We are effectively repeating ourselves at this moment, but we will make our code less repetitive through Meteor.methods later.

Notice how we are using ReactiveVar the same way as we would use a session variable with the difference that we are not exposing the variable to the console. This helps to make the interface a bit more secure.

Let's not forget to add our publishers for this view to work, we will need Products, Orders, and OrderDetails:

```
# /orders/cart/client/order_quantity.coffee

Template.created "order_quantity", ->
  @total = new ReactiveVar()

  @autorun =>
    @subscribe "order_quantity",
      product:FlowRouter.current().params.product
      order:Session.get "global.order"

# /orders/cart/server/order_quantity_pub.coffee

Meteor.publish "order_quantity", (ops={}) ->
  if ops.product and not _.isEmpty ops.product
    @relations
      collection:Products
      filter:
        _id:ops.product

    @relations
      collection:Orders
      filter:
        _id:ops.order
        status:"new"
      mappings:[
```

```
        {
          key:"order"
          collection:OrderDetails
          filter:
            product:ops.product
        }
    ]

    @ready()
```

We learned how to build a custom form using ReactiveVar variables. The topic covers ReactiveVar and touches on Jeet. We learned how to use reactive variables to create rich UX.

Forms

So far, our buttons and forms have been highly inefficient because they are not easy to repeat, and therefore, not easy to maintain. There are two ways that we can use to make our code easier to manage:

- Meteor Methods
- Autoform

With Meteor Methods, we can easily create **repeatable** and **secure** functions while autoforms can identify the structure of a collection and generate form elements from it. This provides a decent layer of security without much effort as well. Autoform and Meteor Methods can be used together as well for further security.

The autoform method can be implemented through the `aldeed:autoform` and `aldeed:collection2` packages.

Meteor Methods

Meteor Methods can be used on the client or the server. They are created by using the `Meteor.methods(<object-of-functions>)` function and run with the `Meteor.call(<function-name>, <callback function>)` function. Running a meteor method from the client causes 2 versions of the same function to run. One runs on the server and manipulates data while the other runs on the client and simulates data manipulation. This is what we call a Method Stub. Let's look at some example code to understand this concept:

```
# Define your method CLIENT SIDE
Meteor.methods
```

```coffee
  say_hello: ->
    console.log "hello"

# Define your method SERVER SIDE
Meteor.methods
  say_hello: ->
    console.log "I don't want to say hello"

# Run the function CLIENT SIDE
Meteor.call "say_hello"
```

Once you run the function, the Meteor Method activates both the server-side and client-side functions. So the server in this case will log "I don't want to say hello" to the console while the client will log "hello". This is a special feature that Meteor provides to help validate code or run other functions in parallel on the server without exposing sensitive data to the client.

Still, it is important to note that the client-side method will run immediately while the server-side method will take longer. The client-side code should, therefore, be used for simulation while the server-side code should be used for validation.

Let's define and use a Meteor Method that runs on both the client and the server. Let's start by redefining the add-to-cart events that we had programmed earlier:

```coffee
# /orders/cart/cart_methods.coffee

Meteor.methods
  "cart.add-to-cart": (ops={},callback) ->
    #ops
      # order
      # product
      # quantity

    order = Orders.findOne ops.order
    product = Products.findOne ops.product

    # Insert Order if it doesn't exist
    unless order
      order_id = Orders.insert
        status:"new"
        total_products:0
        subtotal:0
        total:0
    else
      order_id = order._id
```

```
# Set the session variable for future reference
if Meteor.isClient
  Session.setPersistent "global.order",order_id

# Find the order
order = Orders.findOne order_id

# Check for details on this product
detail = OrderDetails.findOne
  product:product._id
  order:order._id

if detail
  # Increase by one if the details exist
  OrderDetails.update detail._id,
    $inc:
      quantity:ops.quantity

  Orders.update order._id,
    $inc:
      total_products:ops.quantity
      subtotal:product.price * ops.quantity
      total:product.price * ops.quantity
else
  # Insert if details do not exist
  OrderDetails.insert
    quantity:ops.quantity
    product:product._id
    order:order._id

  Orders.update order._id,
    $inc:
      total_products:ops.quantity
      subtotal:product.price * ops.quantity
      total:product.price * ops.quantity

# Run the callback function if it exists
callback and callback(null, true)
```

Notice that we have modified the way that we are setting our persistent session variable. The server does not have a session object, so we need to make sure that this snippet of code only runs on the client using `Meteor.isClient`. We have modified the rest of our code to accept quantity, a product ID, and an order ID, which is all we need to be able to manage both the events.

Also, we added a line at the end of the method to check for a callback function and run it, if it exists. Observe how we have accepted a function as one of our parameters in the beginning of the function. To follow in Meteor's footsteps, we return `null` as the error object and `true` as the result after the function has completed. Now let's replace the events:

```coffee
# /orders/cart/client/order_quantity.coffee

# Attach a reactive variable to the instance
# this variable controls our total
Template.created "order_quantity", ->
  ...


Template.order_quantity.helpers
  ...


Template.order_quantity.events
  ...

  "click .add-to-cart": (event,i) ->
    # Get the total
    total = i.total.get()
    unless total
      return
    else
      total = Number total

    Meteor.call "cart.add-to-cart",
      order:Session.get "global.order"
      product:FlowRouter.current().params.product
      quantity:total
      (error,r) ->
        if not error
          FlowRouter.go "products"
```

```coffee
# /products/client/product.coffee

Template.created "product", ->
  ...


Template.product.events
  "click button.add-to-cart": (event) ->
    Meteor.call "cart.add-to-cart",
      order:Session.get "global.order"
```

```
product:@_id
quantity:1
(error,r) ->
  if not error
    FlowRouter.go "products"
```

Meteor Methods are great to create rich and easily repeatable user interfaces, but you will eventually find yourself repeating certain patterns if you are only updating a single collection. This is where autoforms come in.

Autoform

The `autoform` plugin was installed together with the `collection2` plugin. Both of these work together to quickly create forms that support error handling for you. Documentation on these plugins is vast, but it is necessary to read this to make your views safe and easy to build. You can find this documentation at `https://github.com/aldeed/meteor-autoform`. We are going to cover a simple pattern to show you how to easily manipulate autoforms.

To use autoform, you need to first create a `collection2` schema for your collection. This defines the rules that autoform is going to use to validate and generate our input fields. Let's populate our products schema:

```
# /_globals/lib/collections/products/products_collection.coffee

@Products = new Mongo.Collection "products"

Products.attachSchema new SimpleSchema
  name:
    type:String
    label:"Name"

  description:
    type:String
    label:"Description"
    optional:true

  sku:
    type:String
    label:"SKU"
    optional:true

  price:
    type:Number
    label:"Price"
```

In this snippet of code, we are defining every field within a `new SimpleSchema` constructor, then we have attached the schema to the collection using the `.attachSchema` function. The `SimpleSchema` constructor takes an object where the first key defines the name of the field and the object within that key defines the way the field will behave. We will dive into this further in the next chapter.

Attaching a schema to our collections makes sure that the client-side console commands cannot add information to the database that is not a part of the schema. Let's reset our project to make sure our new products adapt to the new schema:

```
meteor reset
```

Now we can create a simple insert form for our products collection using autoforms. Let's create the template and route:

```jade
//- /products/client/create_product.jade

template(name="create_product")
  h3.text-center create product

  div.container
    div.row
      div.col-xs-12
        +autoForm collection="Products" type="insert" id="insert_
product" preserveForm="true"
          +afQuickField name="name" autocorrect="off"
autocomplete="off"
          +afQuickField name="price"
          +afQuickField name="description"
          +afQuickField name="sku"

          button.btn.btn-block.btn-primary Add Product
```

```coffee
# /products/products_route.coffee

FlowRouter.route "/",
  ...

FlowRouter.route "/products/create",
  name:"create_product"
  action: ->
    FlowLayout.render "layout",
      content:"create_product"
```

Notice that we do not need to write a controller to make this work. There are two critical components that we need to understand in this case: autoForm and afQuickField.

When we use autoForm with a collection, we have to declare the name of the collection using the collection parameter. Also, we need to define whether the form is doing an insert, update, or method call using the type parameter, and finally, we give the form an id that will be used as the HTML id attribute for the form. Additionally, we pass the preserveForm parameter to make sure that the data persists through hot code reloads. There are several other parameters that autoform takes, but these are the most commonly used.

The afQuickField component specifically creates a bootstrap3 input field that can easily handle errors. Notice that we can add HTML attributes (such as autocorrect and autocomplete) to these components as well as parameters. There are a variety of ways to customize these inputs but we recommend only two: modifying the CSS directly or leveraging afFieldInput and afFieldIsInvalid to build new elements.

Let's customize our price field a little bit more:

```
div.form-group(class="{{#if afFieldIsInvalid name='price'}} has-
error has-feedback {{/if}}")

  label.control-label {{afFieldLabelText name="price"}}

  +afFieldInput name="price" validation="submit"

  if afFieldIsInvalid name="price"
    span.glyphicon.glyphicon-certificate.form-control-feedback
    span.help-block {{afFieldMessage name="price"}}
```

By doing this, we are very easily adding a glyphicon to our field using bootstraps' classes, but this can be useful for adapting our forms to any framework, if needed.

There is still a bit of an issue with this form though, people input prices in dollars instead of cents, but our schema only accepts cents. Let's transform this data before it is submitted using autoform's **hooks**:

```
# /products/client/create_product.coffee

AutoForm.addHooks "insert_product",
  formToDoc: (product) ->
    product.price = product.price * 100

    product
```

```
docToForm: (product) ->
  product.price = product.price / 100

  product
```

Autoform has a long list of hooks, but by far the most useful one for transformations is `formToDoc`. This function runs every time the form is converted to a document for processing, this includes before the errors are processed. We do not use the "before hook" because this hook will run after processing errors. Also, we are using a `docToForm` hook to make sure that our `price` field stays intact after a code reload. Autoform has the following hooks:

```
before:
  insert:
  update:
  update-pushArray:
  method:
  method-update:
  normal:
after:
  insert:
  update:
  update-pushArray:
  method:
  method-update:
  normal:
onSubmit:
onSuccess:
onError:
formToDoc:
formToModifier:
docToForm:
beginSubmit:
endSubmit:
```

With this, we can quickly create forms and modify them to the way we like while preserving usability. Stay away from fields that require arrays! They are difficult to manage in our application and can always be expressed as a new collection in our models.

Loading data

The performance of our frontend can suffer if we do not load data correctly because it can make the DOM redraw quickly multiple times. If the calculations are complex, then we need to wait for all our data to be available and calculate everything in one single sweep. If we do not wait for data, then calculations will run as the data is received, which in turn will cause the DOM to redraw multiple times very quickly.

To solve this issue, we can easily check whether our subscribers are ready and show a loading symbol until they are.

Designing the loading indicator

We start by creating a loading template. Let's use font awesome to handle our animations and make sure that we can easily change the color of the loader:

```
//- /loader/loader.jade
```

```
template(name="loader")
  div#loader.template
    div(class="{{color_class}}").vertical-align.text-center
      i.fa.fa-5x.fa-cog.fa-spin
```

```
// /loader/loader.styl
```

```
#loader
  height:100%
```

In this case, we are using the `fa-spin` class to make the cog spin and adding a `color_class` helper that will take bootstraps' `text-` classes to define colors. Also, we made sure that the loader fills the contents of whatever is holding it so that everything aligns nicely when we use it.

Implementing the loading indicator

Let's implement the loading indicator for our list of products. Due to the way we are going to implement this, we could easily have our interface show the loading indicator for each product or the list of products. It will be more efficient to control the latter.

So let's modify our products template:

```
//- /products/client/products.jade
```

```
template(name="products")
```

```
div#products.template
  header#promoter
    ...

  section#features
    ...

  section#featured_products
    div.container
      div.row
        if Template.subscriptionsReady
          each products
            +product
        else
          div(style="height:160px;")
            +loader color_class="text-primary"

  br
```

Meteor core exposes a special `Template.subscriptionsReady` helper that checks whether the subscriptions made in that template instance are all in the ready state. This is one of the hidden advantages of using `@subscribe` from our `Template.created` function instead of `Meteor.subscribe`.

In this case, we only run the `each` iteration on the `products` variable until all subscriptions are ready. Before this happens, we render our `loader` component in our primary color.

The advantage to this pattern is that we can control exactly where we want our loader to be and when we want it to appear.

Animations and transitions

Animation for the web is a vast field that is still growing and can get highly complex if you want it to be. At the end of the day though, efficient animations are what make a real difference. How do you make an animation efficient? You keep it simple, and you let the browser animate it for you. Stay away from using JavaScript to identify positions and change colors. Animations that are heavy on JavaScript will always have terrible performance. This poor performance happens because JavaScript cannot run effectively in all devices, so multiple changes to the DOM occur at the maximum allowed speed of the device without using video memory.

Canvas is an HTML element that is designed to render changes using JavaScript and WebGL. Animating anything through canvas will boost performance, but it is meant more for applications that want to do graphically intensive work such as 3D rendering or sprite animations for a game. We will not cover canvas in this book because you will probably never need it.

Ignoring the power of canvas leaves us with two CSS tools to make rich animations: `animation` and `transition`. The `animation` property is meant for complex animations that require keyframes, while the `transition` property is meant for simple change-of-state animations. Let's look at an example of each to first understand how they work, then we will apply them to Meteor.

Animating with CSS

The `transition` property is the easiest property to understand. You basically define which property you are going to animate and how, within a CSS property:

```
.box
    transition: <CSS property> <duration> <timing function> <delay>
```

It's important to realize that because of **Stylus Nib** (another useful Stylus plugin included in this package), we do not have to worry about vendor prefixes for this particular property. Nib will handle this for us automatically. By adding the transition property to the box class, we are telling the browser to animate any change that occurs on the defined property. How do these changes occur? With new classes. Let's look at a small example:

```
.box
  transition: opacity 300ms ease-in
  opacity: 0
  .in
    opacity: 1
```

With this set of CSS rules, we are making the box invisible until the `.in` class is dynamically added. Once the class is added, then the DOM element will fade in. The available timing functions are: `ease`, `linear`, `ease-in`, `ease-out`, `ease-in-out`, `step-start`, and `step-end`.

The `animation` property is a bit more complex because it does not require a dynamic class to activate the animation:

```
.box
  animation:
    <animation name>
    <duration>
```

```
        <timing function>
        <delay>
        <direction>
        <iteration count>
        <fill mode>
        <play state>

    @keyframes <animation name>
      0%
        background:blue
      50%
        background:green
      100%
        background:red
```

As you can see, the difference between a transition and an animation is the level of control you can have over the animation. By using an `animation name` and the `@keyframes` selector, we can control at which point of the animation we want our properties to change and to what. You can change the number on the keyframe to whatever number you want.

Notice that the `animation` property has a few new parameters: `iteration count`, `fill mode`, and `play state`. The `iteration count` parameter defines how many times an animation is going to play; you can set this to infinite or a specific number. The `fill mode` defines the state at which you want the element to be when it is not animating: `forwards` sets values to the last defined keyframe, `backwards` to the first defined keyframe, both sets to `first` and `last`, and `none` will do nothing (default). The `play state` controls whether an animation is playing or not (paused or running).

We can use a second CSS selector to control our `play state`, if we need to in the same way that we did for our `transition` property.

Executing animations in Meteor

In Meteor, it is very easy to control the classes that are rendered on the DOM using helpers, so we can quickly inject a class that will trigger our CSS animation. We will have issues when we want to trigger animations on elements that do not exist in the DOM.

For example, once our products have loaded, they just pop in. What if we want to make the list fade in and the loader fade out instead? This is where Meteor's hidden `@_uihooks` function comes into play.

At the time of writing, this feature is in beta and is still a bit buggy. The best way to handle all the issues that this is causing is through the `percolate:momentum` package. This avoids the need to understand the issues that `uihooks` currently has and how to get around them.

The `momentum` package is designed to intercept Blaze by using the `@_uihooks` function that is made available in the context of the `Template.rendered` function. It is very easy to use and comes packaged with VelocityJS, a jQuery plugin that handles transitions somewhat effectively. We can use a combination of both to help keep things simple.

To customize momentum, we need to register momentum plugins that handle the three hooks that can occur in our DOM: `insertElement`, `removeElement`, and `moveElement`.

`insertElement`	Occurs when a DOM element is created
`removeElement`	Occurs when a DOM element is destroyed
`moveElement`	Occurs when a DOM element is moved from it's DOM location (sorting can cause this to be triggered)

Let's build the plugin named `fade-fast` that will control the fading in and out of our loading indicator of our products:

```
# /_globals/client/momentum/fade-fast.coffee

Momentum.registerPlugin 'fade-fast', (options) ->
  insertElement: (node, next) ->
    $(node)
      .addClass "animate opacity invisible"
      .insertBefore(next)

    Meteor.setTimeout ->
        $(node).removeClass "invisible"
      ,250

  removeElement: (node) ->
    $(node).velocity opacity:0, 250, "easeOut", ->
      $(this).remove()
```

We use the `node` variable to modify the elements that we are going to inject into the DOM, and we always use `insertBefore` with the `next` variable as a parameter to render. Notice that in this case, when we insert, we are adding three classes before the items are rendered to the DOM, and then after 250 milliseconds, we remove the invisible class.

When an element is removed, we will use `velocity` to modify `opacity` and bring this down to `0` in exactly `250` milliseconds. Velocity takes in a callback command that we will use to finally remove the element from the DOM.

Now we can add our styles and place the helper inside our view:

```
//- /products/client/products.jade

    ...

    section#featured_products
      div.container
        div.row
          +momentum(plugin="fade-fast")
            if Template.subscriptionsReady
              each products
                div.col-xs-12.col-sm-4.col-md-3
                  +product
            else
              div(style="height:160px;")
                +loader color_class="text-primary"
```

```
// _globals/client/main.styl

.vertical-align
  ...

.animate
  &.opacity
    transition: opacity 500ms
    opacity:1

    &.invisible
      opacity:0
```

Notice that we have added a `momentum(plugin="fade-fast")` component that defines which plugin to use around the area that is going to render elements with animations. Then we create the classes that will use CSS transition to make each DOM element fade in.

SEO

Meteor has one big problem. It does not support server-side rendering out of the box. This means that robots don't know how to parse our pages because the server does not render the page, the client does! There are many ways to solve this issue. You can try using `meteorhacks:ssr` to enable server-side rendering or you can let a service automate this for you for free. We are going to use a service to keep things simple.

Prerender.io

Meet prerender.io, the easiest way to get your site parsed. Prerender.io is mostly a free service that understands exactly how to parse your page. It basically navigates to your `webapp` and parses each page, and then when a bot hits our `webapp`, our server will fetch the parsed page from prerender.io and respond with this instead.

The service is free for the webapps that have a minimal number of pages that get hit by bots. The more dynamic and the more pages you have, the higher the price will be, but this is unlikely unless you are building a highly dynamic public web page. Even then, the `prerender.io` project can be downloaded and set up personally (so it's still free).

We have installed the `dfischer:prerenderio` package to easily set up the service. The only thing that is left is for us is to authorize. First, go to `www.prerender.io` and open an account, then click the **INSTALL TOKEN** tab on their navbar, and copy your token. Now paste your token under the configuration file:

```
# /_globals/server/prerenderio.coffee
```

```
prerenderio.set "prerenderToken","<yourtoken>"
```

Simple! Your site is now crawl-able. Now let's configure our router to work with prerender and add a 404 page:

```
# /router/config.coffee
```

```
if Meteor.isClient
  Template.created ->
    except = [
      "Template.__dynamicWithDataContext"
      "Template.__dynamic"
      "Template.layout"
      "Template.layout"
      "body"
    ]
```

```
      unless _.contains except, @view.name
        window.prerenderReady = false

        if @subscriptionsReady()
          window.prerenderReady = true

  FlowRouter.notFound =
    action: ->
      FlowLayout.render "layout",
        content:"not_found"
```

Notice that we are creating a global `Template.created` hook function and setting `prerenderReady` to `false` by default. Then, we check whether our subscriptions are ready using `@subscriptionsReady()` and set `prerenderReady` to `true`. It's important to understand that `@subscriptionsReady()` only checks for subscriptions made through `@subscribe` within the template!

Also, notice that we are creating a list of exceptions. This is to ensure that we only check for subscribers on templates that need them.

This pattern ensures prerender does not cache the page until it has actually loaded all the data. Why not use `FlowRouter` global triggers? Sadly, these triggers do not have access to the template instance that is being rendered (since there can be many). If you need more control, you can set this per route/template.

Let's work on our 404 page template:

```
//- /router/client/not_found.jade
```

```
template(name="not_found")
  div#not_found.template
    div.text-center.vertical-align
      h3 404!
      h5 Page not found!
```

To make sure our 404 page prints out the correct 404 response, we are going to have to use `Meta`.

Using Meta

To control prerender, we need to use the `yasinuslu:blaze-meta` package. This package basically injects a template to our `head` HTML tag so that we can easily set tags. Prerender uses tags to identify whether the page should respond with a 404. We can use Meta to set our title, description, keywords, and robots properties as well. Let's start by making our 404 page respond with a 404:

```
# /router/client/not_found.coffee

Template.rendered "not_found", ->
  Meta.set [
    {
      name:"name"
      property:"prerender-status-code"
      content:"404"
    }
    {
      name:"name"
      property:"robots"
      content:"noindex, nofollow"
    }
  ]
```

The `Meta` object has only four functions: `set`, `setTitle`, `unset`, and `config`. It is unlikely that you will use `unset` because metatags do not persist through routes. Both the `set` and `unset` functions require an array of objects, and each object requires all the three keys: `name`, `property`, and `content`.

In the preceding example, we are setting `prerender-status-code` to `404` and `robots` to `noindex, nofollow`. With this, we ensure that our 404 page in fact returns a 404 error and that crawlers do not index the page.

Also, we need to configure `Meta` so that the name of the page is always correct:

```
# /router/config.coffee

if Meteor.isClient
  Meta.config
    options:
      title:"Crashing Meteor"
      suffix:""

  ...
```

Since `Meta` is controlling our `title` tag, we need to remove that tag from `layout.jade`.

Schema.org

Now that our site is crawl-able, we want our products to shine for search engines. Let's upgrade our products to enable Rich Snippets. Rich Snippets follow schema. org standards to build structured data for search engine crawlers such as Google to interpret. With this information, search engines can present your data on their site more prominently, make searches more effective, and even use it in other services. Following their guidelines is a good idea because Google uses these guidelines for its crawler.

To do this, all we need to do is set as many schema.org's properties as possible on our product page. Visit `http://schema.org/Product` for a full list of the available properties. The properties that are most used are:

Property	Type	Description
name (required)	Text	The name of the product
image	URL	The URL of the product
description	Text	The description of the product
offers	OFFER OBJECT	This includes multiple parameters that define the price of the object
price (required)	Number	The price of the product
priceCurrency (required)	Text (ISO 4217) [ex: USD]	The currency of the price

Now let's put this to practice using the `MicroData` spec:

```
//- /products/client/product.jade

template(name="product")
  article#product(itemscope itemtype="http://schema.org/Product")
    h5(itemprop="name") {{name}}

    div.offer(itemprop="offers" itemscope itemtype="http://schema.org/
Offer")
      meta(itemprop="priceCurrency" content="USD")
      span.price(itemprop="price") {{format.money price}}

    button.add-to-cart.btn.btn-block.btn-primary Add 1 to Cart

    button.modify-quantity.btn.btn-block.btn-info Add more to Cart
```

As you can see, to use the `MicroData` spec, you need to add a variety of custom attributes to your view. For the most part, anytime you are going to declare what a particular thing is, you need to express this via the `itemscope` and `itemtype` attributes. When we want to declare properties under this declaration, we need to make sure our DOM elements are children of this declaration and that the property is declared through the `itemprop` attribute.

Summary

This chapter covered several useful patterns that make the implementation of rich and minimal interfaces easy. First, we learned how to use the Twitter Bootstrap framework together with Jeet and Rupture; this improved the way we organize our DOM. Also, we learned how to make super helpers—functions that we can call in both views and controllers.

We took a dive into the different kinds of variables that we can use to keep our code safe and to create rich interfaces. Also, we learned how to use Meteor Methods and autoform to easily save information. We covered how to implement a simple loading indicator and how to get animations working in Meteor. To finish up, we learned how to implement a little SEO using prerender.io and the `Meta` package.

The next chapter will cover application-wide patterns. *Chapter 4*, *Application Patterns* will teach us how to filter and page through collections, how to fully secure our application, and how to integrate with external APIs.

4
Application Patterns

This chapter will cover application-wide patterns that share server- and client- side code. With these patterns, your code will become more secure and easier to manage. You will learn the following topics:

- Filtering and paging collections
- Security
- External API

Filtering and paging collections

So far, we have been publishing collections without thinking much about how many documents we are pushing to the client. The more documents we publish, the longer it will take the web page to load. To solve this issue, we are going to learn how to show only a set number of documents and allow the user to navigate through the documents in the collection by either filtering or paging through them.

Filters and pagination are easy to build with Meteor's reactivity.

Router gotchas

Routers will always have two types of parameters that they can accept: query parameters, and normal parameters. Query parameters are the objects that you will commonly see in site URLs followed by a question mark (`<url-path>?page=1`), while normal parameters are the type that you define within the route URL (`<url>/<normal-parameter>/named_route/<normal-parameter-2>`). It is a common practice to set query parameters on things such as pagination to keep your routes from creating URL conflicts.

A URL conflict happens when two routes look the same but have different parameters. A products route such as /products/:page collides with a product detail route such as /products/:product-id. While both the routes are differently expressed because of the differences in their normal parameter, you arrive at both the routes using the same URL. This means that the only way the router can tell them apart is by routing to them programmatically. So the user would have to know that the FlowRouter.go() command has to be run in the console to reach either one of the products pages instead of simply using the URL.

This is why we are going to use query parameters to keep our filtering and pagination stateful.

Stateful pagination

Stateful pagination is simply giving the user the option to copy and paste the URL to a different client and see the exact same section of the collection. This is important to make the site easy to share.

In *Chapter 2, Publish and Subscribe Patterns* we had created a products publisher and subscriber to elaborate on our publishers. Now we are going to understand how to control our subscription reactively so that the user can navigate through the entire collection.

First, we need to set up our router to accept a page number. Then we will take this number and use it on our subscriber to pull in the data that we need. To set up the router, we will use a FlowRouter query parameter (the parameter that places a question mark next to the URL).

Let's set up our query parameter:

```
# /products/client/products.coffee

Template.created "products", ->
  @autorun =>
    tags = Session.get "products.tags"
    filter =
      page: Number(FlowRouter.getQueryParam("page")) or 0

    if tags and not _.isEmpty tags
      _.extend filter,
        tags:tags

    order = Session.get "global.order"
    if order and not _.isEmpty order
```

```coffee
      _.extend filter,
        order:order


    @subscribe "products", filter

Template.products.helpers
  ...


  pages:
    current: ->
      FlowRouter.getQueryParam("page") or 0



Template.products.events
  "click .next-page": ->
    FlowRouter.setQueryParams
      page: Number(FlowRouter.getQueryParam("page")) + 1

  "click .previous-page": ->
    if Number(FlowRouter.getQueryParam("page")) - 1 < 0
      page = 0
    else
      page = Number(FlowRouter.getQueryParam("page")) - 1

    FlowRouter.setQueryParams
      page: page
```

What we are doing here is straightforward. First, we extend the filter object with a `page` key that gets the current value of the page query parameter, and if this value does not exist, then it is set to `0`. `getQueryParam` is a reactive data source, the `autorun` function will resubscribe when the value changes. Then we will create a helper for our view so that we can see what page we are on and the two events that set the page query parameter.

But wait. How do we know when the limit to pagination has been reached? This is where the `tmeasday:publish-counts` package is very useful. It uses a publisher's special function to count exactly how many documents are being published.

Let's set up our publisher:

```coffee
# /products/server/products_pub.coffee

Meteor.publish "products", (ops={}) ->
  limit = 10
  product_options =
```

```
      skip:ops.page * limit
      limit:limit
      sort:
        name:1

   if ops.tags and not _.isEmpty ops.tags
     @relations
       collection:Tags
       ...
           collection:ProductsTags
           ...
               collection:Products
               foreign_key:"product"
               options:product_options
               mappings:[
                   ...
                 ]

   else
     Counts.publish this,"products",
       Products.find()
       noReady:true

     @relations
       collection:Products
       options:product_options
       mappings:[
           ...
         ]

   if ops.order and not _.isEmpty ops.order
     ...

   @ready()
```

To publish our counts, we used the `Counts.publish` function. This function takes in a few parameters:

```
Counts.publish <always this>,<name of count>, <collection to count>,
<parameters>
```

Note that we used the `noReady` parameter to prevent the `ready` function from running prematurely. By doing this, we generate a counter that can be accessed on the client side by running `Counts.get "products"`. Now you might be thinking, why not use `Products.find().count()` instead? In this particular scenario, this would be an excellent idea, but you absolutely have to use the `Counts` function to make the count reactive, so if any dependencies change, they will be accounted for.

Let's modify our view and helpers to reflect our counter:

```coffee
# /products/client/products.coffee

...

Template.products.helpers
  pages:
    current: ->
      FlowRouter.getQueryParam("page") or 0

    is_last_page: ->
      current_page = Number(FlowRouter.getQueryParam("page")) or 0

      max_allowed = 10 + current_page * 10
      max_products = Counts.get "products"

      max_allowed > max_products
```

```jade
//- /products/client/products.jade

template(name="products")
  div#products.template
    ...
      section#featured_products
        div.container
          div.row
            br.visible-xs
            //- PAGINATION
            div.col-xs-4
              button.btn.btn-block.btn-primary.previous-page
                i.fa.fa-chevron-left

            div.col-xs-4
              button.btn.btn-block.btn-info {{pages.current}}
```

```
      div.col-xs-4
        unless pages.is_last_page
          button.btn.btn-block.btn-primary.next-page
            i.fa.fa-chevron-right

      div.clearfix
      br

      //- PRODUCTS
      +momentum(plugin="fade-fast")
            . . .
```

Great! Users can now copy and paste the URL to obtain the same results they had before. This is exactly what we need to make sure our customers can share links. If we had kept our page variable confined to a `Session` or a `ReactiveVar`, it would have been impossible to share the state of the webapp.

Filtering

Filtering and searching, too, are critical aspects of any web app. Filtering works similar to pagination; the publisher takes additional variables that control the filter. We want to make sure that this is stateful, so we need to integrate this into our routes, and we need to program our publishers to react to this. Also, the filter needs to be compatible with the pager. Let's start by modifying the publisher:

```
# /products/server/products_pub.coffee

Meteor.publish "products", (ops={}) ->
  limit = 10
  product_options =
    skip:ops.page * limit
    limit:limit
    sort:
      name:1

  filter = {}

  if ops.search and not _.isEmpty ops.search
    _.extend filter,
      name:
        $regex: ops.search
        $options:"i"
```

```coffee
if ops.tags and not _.isEmpty ops.tags
  @relations
    collection:Tags
    mappings:[
        ...
        collection:ProductsTags
        mappings:[
            collection:Products
            filter:filter
            ...
    ]

else
  Counts.publish this,"products",
    Products.find filter
    noReady:true

  @relations
    collection:Products
    filter:filter
    ...

if ops.order and not _.isEmpty ops.order
  ...


@ready()
```

To build any filter, we have to make sure that the property that creates the filter exists and _.extend our filter object based on this. This makes our code easier to maintain. Notice that we can easily add the filter to every section that includes the Products collection. With this, we have ensured that the filter is always used even if tags have filtered the data. By adding the filter to the Counts.publish function, we have ensured that the publisher is compatible with pagination as well.

Let's build our controller:

```coffee
# /products/client/products.coffee

Template.created "products", ->
  @autorun =>
    ops =
      page: Number(FlowRouter.getQueryParam("page")) or 0
      search: FlowRouter.getQueryParam "search"
    ...
```

```
      @subscribe "products", ops

  Template.products.helpers
    ...

    pages:
      search: ->
        FlowRouter.getQueryParam "search"

      ...

  Template.products.events
    ...

    "change .search": (event) ->
      search = $(event.currentTarget).val()

      if _.isEmpty search
        search = null

      FlowRouter.setQueryParams
        search:search
        page:null
```

First, we have renamed our `filter` object to `ops` to keep things consistent between the publisher and subscriber. Then we have attached a `search` key to the `ops` object that takes the value of the search query parameter. Notice that we can pass an undefined value for `search`, and our subscriber will not fail, since the publisher already checks whether the value exists or not and extends filters based on this. It is always better to verify variables on the server side to ensure that the client doesn't accidentally break things. Also, we need to make sure that we know the value of that parameter so that we can create a new `search` helper under the `pages` helper. Finally, we have built an event for the search bar. Notice that we are setting query parameters to `null` whenever they do not apply. This makes sure that they do not appear in our URL if we do not need them.

To finish, we need to create the search bar:

```
//- /products/client/products.jade

template(name="products")
  div#products.template
    header#promoter
      ...
```

```
div#content
  section#features
    ...


  section#featured_products
    div.container
      div.row
        //- SEARCH
        div.col-xs-12
          div.form-group.has-feedback
            input.input-lg.search.form-control(type="text"
placeholder="Search products" autocapitalize="off"
autocorrect="off" autocomplete="off" value="{{pages.search}}")
            span(style="pointer-events:auto;
cursor:pointer;").form-control-feedback.fa.fa-search.fa-2x


      ...
```

Notice that our search input is somewhat cluttered with special attributes. All these attributes ensure that our input is not doing the things that we do not want it to for iOS Safari. It is important to keep up with nonstandard attributes such as these to ensure that the site is mobile-friendly. You can find an updated list of these attributes here at `https://developer.apple.com/library/safari/documentation/AppleApplications/Reference/SafariHTMLRef/Articles/Attributes.html`.

Security

Many packages secure certain parts of the Meteor stack, but even then, you cannot rely on these packages completely. Also, you have to be very careful about the packages you choose! Some packages might intercept core functions to funnel information out of your application. This means that you should always have a look at the source code of the package before you install it.

This topic is usually an oversight to novice Meteor developers, and yet it is one of the most important topics to know about. To secure our webapp we need to:

- Define roles (set distinctions between users)
- Define schemas for every collection (limit how they can modify fields)
- Define deny rules (limit who can modify fields)
- Use methods, when necessary, to check parameters (ensure complex security when needed)
- Set browser policies

Roles

Using roles, just about every web application creates a distinction between users and what they are allowed to do. To help us manage roles easily, we have installed the `alanning:roles` package. With this package, we are going to control who hits our routes and who may modify our collections.

This package makes the `Roles.userIsInRole` function available, which uses a `roles` collection to make sure that the user is in the correct role:

```
Roles.userIsInRole <user-id OR user-object>, [<list of allowed
roles>], <group>
```

Suppose you need to check whether a user is an `admin` or a `manager` before they access a certain function. For this, you will simply do the following:

```
if Roles.userIsInRole Meteor.userId(), ["admin","manager"]
  # allow
```

Let's add an `admin` role to our application. We can start by creating an initialization file that will automatically build our admin user:

```
# /_globals/server/initial_setup.coffee

Meteor.startup ->
  # Users
  if Meteor.users.find().count() is 0
    user = Accounts.createUser
      email:"you@email.com"
      password:"1234"

    Roles.addUsersToRoles user,["admin"]
```

Notice that we are using the `Roles.addUsersToRoles` function to set the new user's role to `admin`, and this takes place on the server side. Always set user roles on the server side. Next, let's build a login route that can be accessed only if you are not already logged in:

```
# /login/login_route.coffee

FlowRouter.route "/login",
  name:"login"
  triggersEnter:[RT.non_user_only]
  action: ->
    BlazeLayout.render "layout",
      content:"login"
```

To make sure roles run at the right moment when our user first hits the site, we need to make sure that `FlowRouter` activates after roles have been loaded. To do this we use `FlowRouter.initialize()` and `FlowRouter.wait()`.

```coffee
# /_globals/router/config.coffee

if Meteor.isClient
  BlazeLayout.setRoot 'body'

  FlowRouter.wait()
  Meteor.startup ->
    # Initialize roles before FlowRouter
    Tracker.autorun (computation) ->
      if Roles.subscription.ready() and not FlowRouter._initialized
        FlowRouter.initialize()
        computation.stop()
```

The `FlowRouter.route` function accepts a `triggersEnter` parameter and a `triggersExit` parameter. This can be used to redirect the user based on roles. Both these parameters are arrays of functions so that many triggers can be added to each route. To make it easier for us, we are going to create a dictionary of triggers under a global RT object. Notice that we do not execute the function within the triggers array, so we do not include parentheses.

Let's start by moving the `/router` folder to the `/_globals` folder. This will make sure that the RT object is the first thing that is defined. After doing this, we should define two triggers:

```coffee
# /_globals/router/triggers.coffee

@RT =
  non_user_only: (context,redirect) ->
    if Meteor.userId()
      if context and context.oldRoute
        redirect context.oldRoute.path
      else
        redirect "/"

  admin_only: (context,redirect) ->
    if not Roles.userIsInRole Meteor.userId(), ["admin"]
      if context and context.oldRoute
        redirect context.oldRoute.path
      else
        redirect "/"
```

Notice that when `FlowRouter` calls these functions, it will include a `context` object and a `redirect` function. The `context` object has information about the route that we are trying to connect to and our previous route, while the `redirect` function is used to redirect a user. In this case, we have attempted to redirect to the previous route if it exists, if it does not exist, then we redirect to root.

Now, let's add the `admin_only` trigger to every route except `products` and `login`:

```coffee
# /_globals/router/triggers.coffee

@RT =
  non_user_only: (context,redirect) ->
    ...

  admin_only: (context,redirect) ->
    ...

FlowRouter.triggers.enter [RT.admin_only],
  except:["products","login","cart","order_quantity"]
```

We can easily create a global trigger that does not apply to the `products` nor the `login` routes using the `FlowRouter.triggers.<enter or exit>` function. We don't have to worry about including our `404` route since by default; it does not run triggers.

To finish up, let's build a custom login page:

```jade
//- /login/client/login.jade

template(name="login")
  div#login.template
    div.vertical-align.container
      div.row
        div.col-xs-12.col-sm-6.col-sm-offset-3
          form.login
            div.form-group
              label Email
              input.email.input-lg.form-control.text-
center(type="text" placeholder="email" value="{{email}}"
autocapitalize="off" autocorrect="off" autocomplete="off")

            div.form-group
              label Password
              input.password.input-lg.form-control.text-
center(type="password" placeholder="password")
```

```
                    if error
                      div.row
                        div.col-xs-12
                          div.alert.alert-warning {{error}}

                  button.login.btn.btn-block.btn-primary.btn-lg Log In
```

/login/client/login.coffee

```
Template.created "login", ->
  @error = new ReactiveVar false

Template.login.events
  "submit .login": (event,i) ->
    event.preventDefault()
    email = $(".email").val()
    pw = $(".password").val()

    # Check Email
    if email and not _.isEmpty email.trim()
      email = email.replace /\s/g,""
      email = email.trim().toLowerCase()
    else
      i.error.set "Email is invalid"
      return

    # Check Password
    if not pw or _.isEmpty pw
      i.error.set "Password is invalid"
      return

    i.error.set false

    Meteor.loginWithPassword email, pw, (error) ->
      if not error
        i.error.set false
        $("input").val ""
        FlowRouter.go "dashboard"
      else
        i.error.set error.reason

Template.login.helpers
  "error": ->
    Template.instance().error.get()
```

Here, we have used Meteor's core `Meteor.loginWithPassword` function to log in, and we have kept a track of the errors using a `ReactiveVar` variable.

Collection2

Suppose a malicious user visits the site and quickly identifies one of our collections in the browser console. They are going to update one of the products by calling the `Products.update` function. Because our site is insecure, they can successfully call something like this:

```
# Malicious User
Products.update("productid",{$set:{you:"have been modified"}})
```

This will successfully create a field that should not exist for that particular product!

With the `aldeed:collection2` package, we are going to secure our collections by white-listing fields. This makes sure that the allowed users can only set acceptable values on our collections and that these values meet certain criteria.

A `collection` field can take the following parameters:

Parameter	Use
type	This defines the type of the value. This can be any JavaScript primitive: `String`, `Number`, `Boolean`, `Date`, `Object`, or an array of primitives such as `[Object]`, `[String]`.
decimal	This is only available if `type:Number`. This defines whether a number is a decimal. This can be `true` or `false`.
optional	This defines whether the field is required on insert. This can be `true` or `false`.
regEx	This checks whether the string matches the defined `regEx` expression. This can be any `regEx` expression such as `/^[A-Z]$/`.
allowedValues	This checks whether the string matches any of the values in an array. This can be only an array of strings such as `["Green","Blue"]`.
blackbox	This allows any combination of values and objects to be placed as values. This can be only `true` or `false`.
denyUpdate	This defines whether the field can be updated. This can be only `true` or `false`.
denyInsert	This defines whether the field can be inserted. If this field is set to `true`, `optional:true` must be set as well. This can be only `true` or `false`.

Parameter	Use
autoValue	This defines the value that the field will take during an operation. This can be a function only.
custom	This defines the custom function that will validate the field. This can be a function only.
unique	This defines whether the value of the field should be unique. This can be only true or false.

With these parameters, it is easy to lock down every collection including the Meteor.users collection and increase the security of our app drastically.

As we will save all our numerical data in hundreds, we will never use the decimal parameter. You should always avoid decimals regardless of whether you are dealing with money or not.

Both the autoValue and custom parameters expose variables and functions within their context that are critical to understand:

Context variables and functions	Use
this.isInsert	Boolean. This checks whether the field is being inserted.
this.isUpdate	Boolean. This checks whether the field is being updated.
this.upsert	Boolean. Check whether the field is being upserted.
this.userId	String. This checks the current userId. Returns undefined, if it does not exist and is null for all server-initiated functions.
this.isFromTrustedCode	Boolean. This checks whether the field is being modified by the server-side code.
this.isSet	Boolean. This checks whether the field is being modified.
this.value	Anything. If this.isSet, then this will be the value of the field.
this.operator	String. If this.isSet and this.isUpdate, then this will be the operator that modifies the value ($pull, $push, $addToSet, $set, and so on).
this.field("<field-name>")	This is a function that returns an object. This gets the object representation of a field that is being modified. From this object, you can use isSet, value, and operator to get more information. For example, this.field("name").value will return the value of the field name, if it is set.

With these functions, we can add custom validators and custom automatic values depending on the state of the modification. Also, we can check what the values of other fields are and react to them if we need to. If your validation requires complex queries with other collections, DO NOT RELY ON THIS PACKAGE!. This tool is strictly to control collection-specific values and not relationships. Remember that not all our collections are available on the client side, and therefore, are incapable of being validated properly. We will address these kinds of validations in the next topic.

Let's secure all our collections. We will only show the Orders and OrderDetails collections schemas:

```coffee
# /_globals/lib/collections/orders/orders_collection.coffee

@Orders = new Mongo.Collection "orders"

Orders.attachSchema new SimpleSchema
  status:
    type:String
    allowedValues:["new","pending","complete"]

  total_products:
    type:Number

  subtotal:
    type:Number

  tax_total:
    type:Number
    optional:true

  total:
    type:Number

  date_created:
    type:Number
    autoValue: ->
      if @isInsert
        return Date.now()
      if @isUpsert
        $setOnInsert:Date.now()

@OrderDetails = new Mongo.Collection "order_details"
```

```
OrderDetails.attachSchema new SimpleSchema
  order:
    type:String

  product:
    type:String

  price:
    type:Number

  quantity:
    type:Number

  subtotal:
    type:Number

  tax:
    type:Object
    optional:true

  "tax.rate":
    type:Number

  "tax.amount":
    type:Number

  total:
    type:Number
```

As you can see, the pattern for white-listing a field within our collection is a simple object that contains the `Collection2` parameters. Notice that we can define rules for subobjects using MongoDB's dot notation. This means that we can set rules for arrays and object arrays in the same fashion as well:

```
people:
  type:[Object]

"people.$.name":
  type:String

"people.$.age":
  type:Number
```

Still, you do not have to set complex rules often since they are clear indicators that a new collection should be created.

Notice that we are not using any complex custom validation in our schema besides `name` and `type`. Why? Should we check whether the user is an admin, or whether the modification originated from the server-side code, or whether the order belongs to the customer?

While we could start adding a few lists of checks for each field, the true source of the problem stems from allowing users to modify our collection directly from the console. To fully secure our orders, we need to modify the allow/deny rules and use trusted code.

It is important to understand that these schemas are used by server-side code too. This makes sure that neither the client nor the server can mess up our keys.

Deny rules

Now that we know the fields that will be in our collections, we need to make sure that the server allows the right people to modify these collections. To do this, we first need to understand exactly how the allow/deny rules work.

Meteor has two core functions that control whether a collection modification is allowed or not: `Meteor.allow` and `Meteor.deny`.

The `Meteor.allow` functions allow a collection to be modified as soon as one of the rules resolves to `true`. Also, this means that the other allow rules are not evaluated! Knowing this, some developers cram logic into a single allow rule that could easily fail. This is bad practice because the code will be difficult to maintain.

On the other hand, the `Meteor.deny` functions will always run and trump a `Meteor.allow` rule that resolves to `true`. To manage our deny rules effectively, we are going to use the `ongoworks:security` package. With this package, we can easily build reusable and readable rules to be set on our collections.

Let's begin by removing all the allow rules from our project. Then we can set some rules for our `Orders` collection:

`/_globals/lib/collections/orders/server/orders_permissions.coffee`

```
Meteor.startup ->
  # Admin may only modify status
  Orders.permit "update"
    .ifLoggedIn()
```

```
    .ifHasRole "admin"
    .onlyProps "status"
    .apply()
```

With this simple rule, we have denied anything that does not match this rule. This package integrates directly with our `roles` package, so we can easily use the `ifHasRole` function. This rule makes sure that only an admin user can update an order's `status` field via the console. To make sure that the rule is applied, we have used the `apply` function.

There are three things that we need to understand about the deny rules: logic, integrated functions, and custom functions.

Logic in rules decides whether they act as ANDs or ORs. If we have multiple functions inside a rule, then we define AND rules. The function that we have defined for our orders is an AND rule because this checks `ifLoggedIn` AND `ifHasRole` AND `onlyProp` before allowing a modification to pass. If we want to create an OR rule, we simply create a new rule. Let's try this:

```
Orders.permit "update"
    .ifLoggedIn()
    .ifHasRole "admin"
    .onlyProps "status"
    .apply()

Orders.permit ["insert","remove"]
    .never()
    .apply()
```

Here, we are stating that a user may `update` `ifLoggedIn` AND `ifHasRole` AND `onlyProp` OR `never` `insert`/`remove`.

The package comes with a handful of integrated functions to help in applying the rules:

Function	Use
`never()`	This prevents DB operations
`ifLoggedIn()`	This allows DB operations if logged in
`ifHasUserId(<user-id>)`	This allows DB operations if user ID is a particular string
`ifHasRole(<role string>)` `ifHasRole({role:<role string>,group:<group>})`	This allows DB operations if user belongs to a particular role

Function	Use
onlyProps(<string or array of strings>)	This allows DB operations on certain top-level fields only (this will not identify arrays and subobjects)
exceptProps(<string or array of strings>)	This allows DB operations on all top-level fields except these (this will not identify arrays and subobjects)

Custom deny rules

While the security package functions are useful, you may find yourself needing custom functions for more precise handling of your security. To build a custom function, you need to use the Security.defineMethod function:

```
Security.defineMethod <function name>,
  transform:<function>
  deny: <function (type, args, userid, doc, fields, modifier)>
```

This function accepts two parameters: transform and deny. The transform function allows the modification of fields before they enter the deny function, while the deny function is an extended version of Meteor.deny. The deny function passes several arguments that include information about the document being modified and the user. These arguments are: type, arguments, userId, document, fields, and modifier. The last two arguments (fields and modifier) are only passed if type is equal to update.

Let's add a custom function:

```
# /_globals/server/security.coffee

Security.defineMethod "ifUserIsOwner",
  deny: (type,args,user,doc) ->
    user isnt (doc.user or doc._id)
```

Here, we are defining an ifUserIsOwner function that checks whether the ID of the currently logged in user is equal to the user field or the _id field on the modified document.

 Notice that the logic of the rule denies a database operation if the user is not the owner of the document.

Now we can use this rule to secure our `users` collection:

```coffee
# /_globals/server/security.coffee

Security.defineMethod "ifUserIsOwner",
  ...

Security.permit(["update"]).collections([Meteor.users])
  .ifUserIsOwner()
  .onlyProps ["emails"]
  .apply()

Security.permit(["insert","update","remove"]).collections([Meteor.users])
  .ifHasRole "admin"
  .apply()
```

Notice that we are attaching rules to the `Meteor.users` collection in a different way. We do this because the `Meteor.users` collection is a special collection that is initialized in a different way than the rest of our collections, with this we have ensured that the rules are properly attached.

In this example, we are allowing our users freely to modify the `email` field from the console, and only the admin user can modify all users from the console.

However, now that we have locked the code from the client, how are we supposed to make things work? Running code directly from an event on the client will fail because the code is untrusted. We need to build a trusted code that will handle changes to the database. The solution is simple: Meteor methods.

The Meteor methods – round 2

We have already covered how `Meteor.methods` work, but we have not discussed the difference between trusted and untrusted code.

Trusted code can modify multiple documents at once by setting `multi` to `true` and can use an arbitrary Mongo selector to find the documents to modify. It bypasses any access control rules set up by allow and deny. Trusted code includes all server code and `Meteor.methods`.

Untrusted code can modify only a single document at once that is specified by its `_id`. The modification is allowed only after checking any applicable allow and deny rules. Untrusted code cannot perform upserts. Untrusted code includes client code such as event handlers and the console.

This means that whenever we directly modify a collection on the client, we are running untrusted code that is limited by our deny rules. Knowing this, it becomes obvious that most code, especially complex code with relationships, should run on a Meteor method.

But wait. Can a user modify the code of the method on the client side? They most certainly can, but remember that the code runs in a stub. The stub makes sure that the correct code runs on the server, while the client-side code updates the collections temporarily until the server responds. This is what Meteor calls **Optimistic UI**.

So, if someone tampers with the client-side version of our Meteor method, the server-side version will still run normally and the UI will update correctly.

It's important to understand though that `Meteor.methods` will still be bound to the rules we had set on `Collection2`, which is a great feature inside a team environment where not everyone understands the structure of all data models.

So where should we use untrusted code? The answer depends greatly on your application, but for the most part, you will want everything to run on trusted code because it is easier to maintain and safer. Untrusted code should be used mostly to control things that the database is not connected to, or information that is allowed to be just about anything that the user wants.

In order to use `Meteor.methods` properly, we need to run validation on `Meteor.methods` as well. We do this using Meteor's core `check` package. Let's upgrade our `cart.add-to-cart` method:

```
# /orders/cart/cart_methods.coffee

Meteor.methods
  "cart.add-to-cart": (ops={}) ->
    # Validate data
    check ops,
      order:Match.Optional(Match.OneOf(String,null))
      product:String
      quantity:Number

    . . .

    # Insert Order if it doesn't exist
    unless order

      . . .
    else
      # Validate order status
```

```
if order.status isnt "new"
   throw new Meteor.Error 405, "Not Allowed"

order_id = order._id

...
```

First, we have used the `check` function to validate the structure of the `ops` object and to ensure that each key inside the object matches the correct type of data primitive. When the validation fails, the function will automatically stop and return a **404 Match Failed** error to the client.

Next, we have checked the status of the order. If the order is not new, then we throw a `Meteor.Error`. This will short circuit the function as well and return the `error` object to the client. When you are settings errors inside the Meteor methods, you will always use `throw new Meteor.Error(<error message>)` to communicate the error.

We do not need to worry about doing anything else with our errors. We will see how to keep track of our application errors in a different topic.

The `check` function takes only two variables:

```
check <value>, <pattern>
```

The `value` parameter takes the variable that will be analyzed, while the `pattern` parameter takes the validator. The pattern can be as simple as a JavaScript primitive such as `String`, `Number`, and `Boolean`, an array of validators, an object of validators, or as complex as a function. The pattern simply needs to return `true` for the validation to pass.

Meteor includes a handful of useful `pattern` functions through the `Match` object:

Pattern function	Use
`Match.Any()`	This allows any value to pass validation.
`Match.Integer()`	This allows any 32-bit integer. `Infinity` and `NaN` are not allowed.
`Match.ObjectIncluding(<object>:<pattern>)`	This allows an object to include key/value pairs that are not defined in the object. The example that we used does not allow other key/value pairs from entering the method.
`Match.Optional(<second-pattern>)`	This allows a value to be `undefined`. If the value is defined, then the `second-pattern` will be evaluated instead.

Pattern function	Use
`Match.OneOf(<pattern1>, <pattern2>,...)`	This allows a value to pass if it matches any of the defined patterns.
`Match.Where(<function(value){}>)`	This runs `function` and passes the defined value as the first parameter. If the function returns `true`, then validation passes.

Now this is all grand and makes us feel much more secure, but the fact of the matter is that we are sharing our server-side logic on the client. This means that we absolutely cannot include sensitive data inside a Meteor method. If we do want to pass sensitive data, it is best to store it in a server-side variable and call it, or if you want to go an extra mile, you can separate the client-side method from the server using folders.

Managing the wait time

The first chapter gave us a brief explanation of the impact that blocking can have on our client. To summarize this, if a function is waiting for a third-party or doing something that takes long, you should unblock the function. However, what impact can this have?

Remember that methods are placed on a conveyor belt. When we unblock a function, we place the method in a different conveyor belt where we cannot put other methods. This means that if another method depends on the unblocked method to complete, there can be a serious issue because the method can run before, during, or after the unblocked method.

Notice that our `cart.add-to-cart` method does not have an unblock function. This is to make sure that the server adds items to the cart in the same order as the client. So what do we do if we have something inside the method that can be placed in a separate conveyor belt? Can there be something that can happen in parallel and the user does not have to wait to continue?

`Meteor.defer(<function>)` is a special, undocumented function that can take a particular snippet of code and run it in a separate conveyor without blocking the function from which it was called. Suppose we want to notify the admin every time a new order has been created, as shown here:

```
# /orders/cart/cart_methods.coffee

Meteor.methods
  "cart.add-to-cart": (ops={}) ->
```

```
# Validate data
...


# Insert Order if it doesn't exist
unless order
  ...
  if Meteor.isServer
    Meteor.defer ->
      Email.send
        to:"you@email.com"
        from:"me@email.com"
        subject:"New Customer!"
        text:"Someone has created a new order"


  ...
```

In this example, we have wrapped the `Email.send` function in a `Meteor.defer` function to make the e-mail run in parallel. This benefits the performance of your code by running deferred functions in parallel and focusing on producing only the results that matter to the user. By doing this, we ensure that the e-mail, a process that we know takes a long time to finish, does not block the server as well.

Browser policy

Now that we can secure our collections and functions, we need to protect our application as a whole. We can achieve this protection using the `browser-policy` package. Let's install it now:

```
meteor add browser-policy
```

So what exactly does this package do? By adding this, we are opening an access to a series of configuration options that will help us to set our application headers and content security policies to protect from cross-site scripting and data injection attacks.

These kinds of attacks are often used to steal your data (data theft), change the way your site looks (website defacement), and distribute malware. We definitely want to avoid all these attacks.

So how does this work? By adding the package, we have already protected our application against many attacks by default, but we need to be able to control this. To do this, the package exposes two objects each with a particular set of functions: `BrowserPolicy.framing` and `BrowserPolicy.content`. Both these functions must be set in the server.

Framing

With `BrowserPolicy.framing`, we can control whether our web application can be rendered inside an iframe or not. We have three functions to control this:

Function	Use
`*.framing.disallow()`	This will never render in an iframe regardless of the origin.
`*.framing.restrictToOrigin(origin)`	This will only render in iframes created by the specified origin. This may take only one `origin` string and may be called only once. Also, it is not fully supported in WebKit.
`*framing.allowAll()`	This will render in any iframe.

You will find yourself using `BrowserPolicy.framing.disallow()` most of the time, but it is important to understand that you will still be able to iframe your app if origins are the same.

Content

With `BrowserPolicy.content`, we can control exactly how the content will be loaded into our web application. We have many functions for this. However, we will actually end up using only a few. The functions are:

Function	Use
`*.content.allowInlineScripts()`	This allows DOM script tags to run. DEFAULT.
`*.content.disallowInlineScripts()`	This does not allow DOM script tags to run.
`*.content.allowEval()`	This allows the building of JavaScript from strings by using the `eval` function.
`*.content.disallowEval()`	This does not allow the building of JavaScript from strings by using the `eval` function. DEFAULT.
`*.content.allowInlineStyles()`	This allows inline styles and style DOM elements to run. DEFAULT.
`*.content.disallowInlineStyles()`	This does not allow inline styles and style DOM elements to run.

There are more! The next set of functions defines a white-list of content types and how they are allowed to load. `ContentType` can take the value of: `Script`, `Object`, `Image`, `Media`, `Font`, `Frame`, and `Connect`.

Function	Use

`*.allow<ContentType>Origin(origin)`
 	
`*.allowScriptOrigin(origin)`
 	
`*.allowObjectOrigin(origin)`
 	
`*.allowImageOrigin(origin)`
 	
`*.allowMediaOrigin(origin)`
 	
`*.allowFontOrigin(origin)`
 	
`*.allowFrameOrigin(origin)`
 	
`*.allowConnectOrigin(origin)`
	This allows the `ContentType` to be loaded from the `origin` string. This function can be called multiple times and has a support for wildcards. If a protocol (`http` / `https`) is not specified, then BOTH are allowed.

`*.allow<ContentType>DataUrl()`	This allows the `ContentType` to be loaded from a `data:` URL. This will allow base64-encoded images to render.
`*.allow<ContentType>SameOrigin()`	This allows the `ContentType` to be loaded from the same origin as the webapp.
`*.disallow<ContentType>()`	This does not allow `ContentType` to be loaded.
`*.allowSameOriginForAll()`	This allows all types of content to be loaded from the same origin as the webapp.
`*.allowDataUrlForAll()`	This allows all types of content to be loaded from a `data:` URL.
`*.allowOriginForAll(origin)`	This allows all types of content to be loaded from the specified `origin`.
`*.disallowAll()`	This does not allow any type of content to be loaded from anywhere.

Depending on what we want our application to achieve, we may have to tweak our rules. Let's configure our security policy to the recommended options:

```
# /_globals/server/security.coffee
```

```
Meteor.startup ->
  # Prevent webapp from loading on an iframe
  BrowserPolicy.framing.disallow()
```

```coffee
# Prevent inline scripting
BrowserPolicy.content.disallowInlineScripts()

trusted_sites = [
  '*.google-analytics.com'
  '*.mxpnl.com'
  'placehold.it'
  'placeholdit.imgix.net'
]

_.each trusted_sites, (trusted_site) ->
  BrowserPolicy.content.allowOriginForAll
"https://#{trusted_site}"
```

External APIs

Now that we know how to secure our application, we need to understand how to keep external data sources up to date. There are two patterns that we can use to ensure that the information on our server is recent: **synchronization** and **webhooks**.

Synchronization

Synchronization will, basically, get data from our source continuously and refresh the database. This type of technique is useful when we need to save information from our data source and use that information to produce analytical data via the aggregation framework.

To keep our servers synchronized, we need to make sure that the process that fetches information does not block the server. We can ensure that this happens using nonblocking functions like `Meteor.setInterval`.

Let's synchronize with Stripe. First, we will need to create a collection to capture payments, then we will have to set permissions and our Stripe secret, and finally, we will build the HTTP GET function:

```coffee
# /_globals/lib/collections/stripe/payments_collection.coffee

@Payments = new Mongo.Collection "payments"
```

```coffee
# /_globals/lib/collections/stripe/server/payments_permissions.coffee

Meteor.startup ->
  # Nobody may modify
  Payments.permit ["insert","remove","update"]
```

```
    .never()
    .apply()
```

/_globals/server/stripe.coffee

```
@Stripe =
  secret:"secret-key"
  publishable:"publishable-key"
```

/stripe/server/payments.coffee

```
_.extend Stripe,
  get_payments: (ops={}) ->
    params =
      limit:100

    if ops.starting_after_id
      _.extend params,
        starting_after:ops.starting_after_id

    HTTP.get "https://api.stripe.com/v1/charges",
      headers:
        "Authorization":"Bearer #{Stripe.secret}"
      params:params
      (error,result) ->
        if not error
          _.each result.data?.data, (charge) ->
            Payments.upsert _id:charge.id,
              $set:charge

          if result.data.has_more
            last = _.last result.data.data
            Stripe.get_payments
              starting_after_id:last.id

        else
          throw new Meteor.Error error

Meteor.setInterval Stripe.get_payments,3600000
```

Notice that when we created our collection, we did not give it a schema. We did this because we wanted to make sure that our collection is flexible in case the data from our endpoint changes. To secure our collection, we need to make sure that nobody can modify this in any way except for trusted code. Then we have created a configuration object that is going to hold our Stripe secret and public key.

Also, we have created a /stripe/server/payments.coffee directory. Here, we have added the get_payments function to the Stripe object that we had defined in our _globals directory. To have this work properly, we had to pass a params object to control the way we are requesting data from Stripe's servers. Expect to pass params for every GET request you build since this controls the endpoints' pagination. Stripe explains in their documentation that we can get the next page of data by first checking whether there is more data via the has_more key and then passing in the last object ID from which to start via the starting_after parameter.

At the end of this all, we have used the Meteor.setInterval(<function>,<delay in milliseconds>) function to make sure that the function runs every hour. Are we done yet? Not quite. While this code will definitely populate our Payments collection, it could potentially crash our server as well. Why? The request always queries from the beginning of time up to today, which makes the server progressively take longer. Another important issue is that if there is one GET request being processed and it has not finished within the hour, another request could start in parallel and consume even more resources.

We can prevent this by controlling our intervals and limiting the time frame our interval uses to get the data.

First, let's make sure that we only have one interval running at a time:

```
# /stripe/server/payments.coffee

_.extend Stripe,
  payments:
    get: (ops={}) ->
      if not Stripe.payments.is_running
        Stripe.payments.is_running = true

        params =
          limit:100

        if ops.starting_after_id
          _.extend params,
            starting_after:ops.starting_after_id
```

```
        HTTP.get "https://api.stripe.com/v1/charges",
          headers:
            "Authorization":"Bearer #{Stripe.secret}"
          params:params
          (error,result) ->
            if not error
              _.each result.data?.data, (charge) ->
                Payments.upsert _id:charge.id,
                  $set:charge

              if result.data.has_more
                last = _.last result.data.data
                Stripe.payments.get
                  starting_after_id:last.id
              else
                Stripe.payments.is_running = false

            else
              Stripe.payments.is_running = false
              throw new Meteor.Error error

    set_interval: ->
      Meteor.setInterval Stripe.payments.get,360000

    is_running:false


  Stripe.payments.set_interval()
```

Notice that we are keeping payments together under a `payments` object now. Then we have simply set and checked a `is_running` Boolean key to see whether the process is running or not. Now if we were to reduce the interval to 1 millisecond, it would only GET from the external API after the previous request is done processing.

Now, we can use the `starting_after` parameter to ensure that we only get the latest information. To do this, we will have to use the `moment` function to filter data by time and get the latest payment information:

```
# /stripe/server/payments.coffee


_.extend Stripe,
  payments:
    get: (ops={}) ->
      if not Stripe.payments.is_running
        Stripe.payments.is_running = true
```

```
            params =
              limit:100

            if ops.starting_after_id
              _.extend params,
                starting_after:ops.starting_after_id
            else
              date_after =
  moment().utc().startOf("day").subtract(10,"days").unix()
              latest_payment = Payments.findOne
  created:$gte:date_after,
                  sort:
                    created:1

            if latest_payment
              _.extend params
                starting_after:latest_payment.id
          ...
```

In this example, we have simply used moment to identify a Unix timestamp from 10 days ago. The moment object is made available using the momentjs:moment package. Notice that we are using the utc() function to set startOf("day") consistently between our development and production environments. Then we have queried the server, and if the payment exists, we will use the ID of the payment as our starting_after parameter.

It is important to understand that we can make this query easily only because the information that Stripe sends includes a Unix timestamp. Not every API has a Unix timestamp. Most likely, you will end up inserting or transforming their data to fit your own. This can be easily addressed by extending their response when needed.

Webhooks

Webhooks are the way through which other servers can communicate directly with ours. They, basically, make a POST request to one of our endpoints to inform our server that something has happened.

In the case of Stripe, we are going to add an endpoint that will catch all of Stripe's charge webhooks. To do this, we will use the nimble:restivus package.

Restivus is an excellent package that makes it easy to maintain a RESTful API with version control and user authentication. It runs only on the server side for security.

First, we need to create an instance of `Restivus`. This instance will hold the routes for the first version of our endpoint:

```
# /_globals/server/stripe.coffee

@Stripe =
  secret:"secret"
  publishable:"public"
  hooks:
    v1:new Restivus
      apiPath:"stripe"
      version:"v1"
```

Here, we have attached our new server-side endpoint to the global `Stripe` object under the `hooks` and `v1` keys. This will make it easy to create new routes for version 1 anywhere in our server. The `Restivus` instance takes in a handful of parameters, the ones that you will end up using the most are:

Parameter	Use
apiPath	String defines the parent route of all the endpoints. If we define `apiPath` as `"stripe"` and a route as `"charge"`, then the path for the route will be `ROOT_URL/stripe/charge`.
version	String defines the version number of the API and adds it to the parent route. If we define `version` as `"v1"`, then all the routes will take this form: `ROOT_URL/<apiPath>/v1/<route>`.
enableCors	Boolean sets whether the route is accessible from external domains. Default: `true`.

Now let's create an endpoint that updates the `Payments` collection. To create an endpoint, we need to define a route on our `Restivus` instance. To do this, we simply call the global object that we had defined and use the `addRoute` function:

```
# /stripe/server/endpoints/charges.coffee

Meteor.startup ->
  Stripe.hooks.v1.addRoute "charge",
    post: ->
      payment = @request.body.data?.object
      if payment
        Payments.upsert _id:payment.id,
          $set:payment

      @done()
```

Now our endpoint can catch Stripe's webhook notifications. Notice that the information that the POST request contains is located in the @request.body object. After analyzing this object, we can see that the object that Stripe is sending. In this case, Stripe sends an object with a data key, which in turn contains an object key that holds the information of the payment. If you want to see the information that Stripe is responding with, simply log in to the console.

Also, we are returning a @done() function, which notifies Stripe that the request was processed. This makes sure that Stripe does not have to make a second attempt to notify our server.

The addRoute function can handle all types of HTTP requests including get, put, delete, patch, and options. The endpoints have these variables in their context to help handle requests:

Context variable	Use
this.user	The Meteor.user object after authentication passes.
this.userId	The Meteor.userId string after authentication passes.
this.urlParams	Parameters defined in the URL string: ROOT_URL/stripe/v1/charge/:more To access the more parameter, you would call @urlParams.more.
this.queryParams	Query parameters defined in the URL string: ROOT_URL/stripe/v1/charge?more=data To access the more parameter, you would call @urlQueryParams.more.
this.bodyParams	The body of the request. This is the equivalent to @request.body.
this.request	A NodeJS request object.
this.response	A NodeJS response object.
this.done()	This function must be called after handling a response.

Now, we can set up webhooks from Stripe by going to their settings page and creating a webhook. Make sure to point their URL to the one that we built.

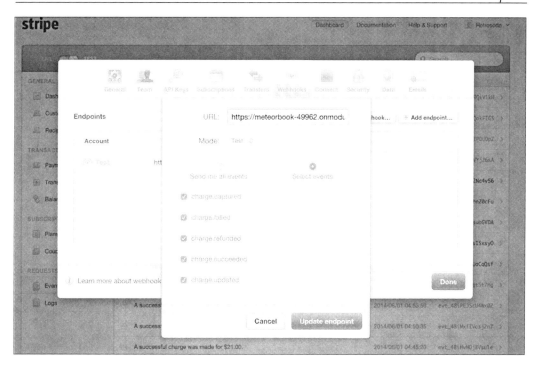

We can send a couple of test hooks, too, to make sure that everything works as intended. By using both the synchronization pattern and the webhooks pattern, we are able to keep our data up to date. You should always use both patterns if the API allows you to. Why? This is because their webhooks server could potentially fail.

Summary

This chapter covered three important things: how to control the amount of data that we publish, how to secure our app, and how to better integrate with an external API. We learned a pattern to build pagination that functions with filters as well. Then we learned how to build user roles and schemas to secure access to our application better. Next, we understood the limitations of allow/deny rules and addressed these limitations by writing effective deny rules. We quickly realized these deny rules were blocking functions from all the event handlers because they are insecure. To get around this limitation, we learned how to build trusted code. Towards the end, integrating Stripe taught us how to create a nonblocking synchronization function and how to use `restivus` to catch incoming messages from external servers.

The next chapter is going to cover the basics of how to test and maintain our code. With the next chapter, we will be able to share our code without fearing that someone else will break it.

5
Testing Patterns

This chapter will cover testing patterns that ensure our code is easy to maintain. With these patterns, you will learn how to implement regression testing—a method to identify if the new code breaks the old code before the code goes into production. Building tests is crucial to maintain code and collaborate with others. You will learn the following topics:

- Behavior tests
- Unit tests

Testing in Meteor is still under heavy development, but the functions that we will cover are basic and are unlikely to change.

Behavior tests

Behavior tests are known as end-to-end tests too. The purpose of a behavior test is simple: it makes sure that a feature of the project is working. A feature refers to the business logic behind the application. For example, a feature of our current project is viewing a list of products in our landing page. Another feature is the ability to add a variable quantity of products to the order.

To run behavior tests in Meteor, we essentially need to build a robot that can visit our website and try to make these features work. While this sounds complex, the Meteor Velocity project simplifies much of this when paired with Cucumber.

Velocity is a project that sets the stage for other testing frameworks to use. It works by creating mirrors of the project where tests can run.

Cucumber is a specification-by-example testing framework. It is meant to describe application features in plain English before they are programmed. In a collaboration setting, these tests are the ones that matter most because they make sure that the application is behaving as expected. We will use the Cucumber package now because it is one of the only testing frameworks that support behavior tests that are currently available to Meteor.

To build tests, we first need to install the `xolvio:cucumber` package:

```
meteor add xolvio:cucumber
```

This package automatically installs Velocity and all other required packages. Now run the Meteor command to start up the server. The following two things are going to happen:

- A new browser window will open if there are any tests to run
- The current project will have a dot on the top-right side

The new browser window is what we call a **mirror** and is the client that is going to run all the behavior tests that we define. While this is great, it is annoying to have a second browser window open and close every time we run the Meteor command.

To get rid of the second browser window, we can use `phantomjs` to run tests. To do this, we will simply run the Meteor command with some settings:

```
SELENIUM_BROWSER=phantomjs meteor
```

PhantomJS is a headless browser. A headless browser is a web browser (such as Safari and Chrome) without a **Graphical User Interface** (**GUI**). In other words, it's a browser for robots, and this is exactly what our robot needs to run our tests.

Let's make a custom Meteor alias with this command. Open the `~/.bash_profile` directory with your favorite text editor. If you use Sublime Text 3, you can run the following command:

```
sublime ~/.bash_profile
```

In this file, add this line to the end of the document:

```
# ~/.bash_profile

alias devmeteor='SELENIUM_BROWSER=phantomjs meteor'
```

Now completely quit your terminal, and then open it again. Go to your project and run the `devmeteor` command to start your project.

Go to the project URL. Here, you will notice a blue circle on the top-right corner of the project. Click this to reveal the velocity test dashboard. Whenever tests fail, here you will see why they failed. All tests are rerun every time there is a change in the code.

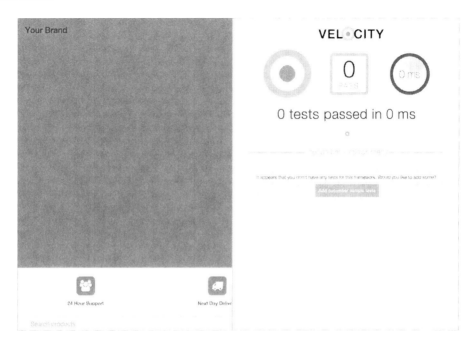

Let's start by building our first behavior test. In this test, we are going to check whether we can add items to the order. To do this, we need to program two key components:

- Features
- Steps

Steps are, basically, snippets of code in JavaScript or CoffeeScript that interpret the **feature**. Step snippets are automatically generated after writing a feature. Therefore, we need to start by writing the description of the feature.

All our tests are going to be saved under the /tests directory. Behavior tests will always go under the /cucumber folder. At the time of this writing book, this has been mandatory because Velocity runs under these special directories only:

```
# /tests/cucumber/features/cart/add to cart.feature

Feature: Add to Cart
```

```
As a customer
I want to add items to my cart
So I can checkout

Background:
  Given I am an anonymous customer

@dev
Scenario: Add one to cart
  When I navigate to "/"
  And I click on the first button with class ".add-to-cart"
  Then I should have one product with quantity 1 in my cart
```

Notice that the file ends in `.feature` and is located under the `/features` directory. Placing files under the `features` directory is mandatory as well for the testing suite to be able to identify your feature files.

This file is written in the Gherkin language. If you want to add comments, you can use the pound sign (#) just we do in CoffeeScript. The `Feature` keyword describes the feature; this can be anything as long as it helps you to identify what the feature is. After this, we can see three lines that describe the purpose of the feature. This description can also be anything you want since this does not affect the test, but it is common to use the following syntax to help identify whether the feature is useful or not:

```
As a [role]
I want [feature]
So that [benefit]
```

Next, we will find the `Background` and `Scenario` keywords. Both are a list of actions that lead to a result. For each feature, there can be multiple scenarios that test the different parts of the feature. The `Background` keyword defines a list of actions to be taken before running the ones under the `Scenario` keyword. Try to keep backgrounds short and simple, and keep in mind that they will run for every scenario.

Also, notice that we have an `@dev` keyword directly above the `Scenario` keyword; this keyword controls where `Scenario` is going to run. If you do not include a keyword, it will only run when you run `meteor --test` in your terminal. If you include `@dev`, the test will run every time you make changes to your web application. Also, you can include `@ignore` to ignore the test completely.

The Given, When, And, and Then keywords are commands that run the steps in our test code:

- Given: The purpose of Given is to put the app in a known state before any interaction occurs.
- When: The purpose of When is to describe the key action the user performs.
- And: The purpose of And is to write scenarios more fluently. They, basically, substitute And with the previous keyword.
- Then: The purpose of Then is to observe and evaluate outcomes. This phrase will always make sure that the system has produced something.

Now that we have programmed our first feature, let's generate the steps that will execute the feature. Run your alias command:

```
devmeteor
```

Once the server has started, Velocity will produce a command you can use to tail the projects' cucumber.log. Open up a separate terminal without deactivating Meteor and run that command. It should look something like this:

```
tail -f /Users/YOU/pathtoyourproject/online_shop/.meteor/local/log/
cucumber.log
```

Now you will see something like this:

If you don't, you can restart the Meteor project without leaving `cucumber.log`. Here, we can see the JavaScript version of the steps that the feature is expecting. Let's rewrite these in CoffeeScript under the special `/step_definitions` directory. This directory must always be a sibling to the related `.feature` files.

Copy the code snippets and create a new file under the `/tests/cucumber/features/cart/step_definitions/steps.coffee` directory. We are going to convert these snippets to CoffeeScript, since this is what we have been working with all along. You can do this quickly at `http://js2.coffee`.

Notice that each function passes a `callback` variable at the end and calls the `pending()` function. When tests run, this indicates that the function has not been built yet and appears as pending in the Cucumber log. We can remove the `callback` variable after we have finished working with the function. Notice that arguments are passed as well.

Running tests with this code will not work; we need to initialize the test properly. To do this, we begin by using CoffeeScripts' do function and attaching the commands to the `module.exports` function. You need to do this for every test file:

```
# /tests/cucumber/features/cart/step_definitions/steps.coffee

do ->
  'use strict'

  module.exports = ->
    @Given ...
    @When ...
    @Then ...
```

Now that the tests are actually running, we can dive deeper. The first function that we will address is `Given`. `Given` needs to make sure that the user is completely new and has no active order. To do this, we are going to use **fixtures**. Fixtures are `Meteor.methods` exclusively available in testing. We can use these methods to clear our database or add seed data. Let's start by making a fixture that ensures that the user is anonymous and another fixture that clears all the orders:

```
# /tests/cucumber/fixtures/cart_fixtures.coffee

do ->
  'use strict'

  Meteor.methods
    "anonymous_user": ->
```

```
      if @userId
        @setUserId null

    "reset_orders": ->
      Orders.remove {}
      OrderDetails.remove {}
```

Now, we can call these methods in the `Given` function (or any other function) using the `@server.call` function:

```coffee
# /tests/cucumber/features/cart/step_definitions/steps.coffee

do ->
  'use strict'

  module.exports = ->
    @Given /^I am an anonymous customer$/, ->
      @server.call "reset_orders"
      @server.call "anonymous_user"
```

Notice that we are using `@server`, but we can use `@client` too since this is a call to `Meteor.method`. Now let's program `When`:

```coffee
# /tests/cucumber/features/cart/step_definitions/steps.coffee

do ->
  'use strict'
  ...

  module.exports = ->
    url = require('url')
    @Given /^I am an anonymous customer$/, ->
        ...

    @When /^I navigate to "([^"]*)"$/, (path) ->
      @browser
        .url url.resolve(process.env.ROOT_URL, path)

    @When /^I click on the first button with class "([^"]*)"$/,
    (button) ->
      @browser
        .waitForExist "body *"
        .waitForVisible ".product"
        .element ".product:nth-child(1) #{button}"
        .click()
```

The `@browser` object gives access to an instance of webdriver. This means that we can use the webdriver functions to simulate user clicks, inspect elements, and browse the Web. Notice that we can require NPM modules through the `require` function as well. In this case, we will require the `url` module to help identify routes.

The first `When` function requires a single argument defined by the regular expression. In this case, it is the `path` variable. Arguments will always be listed one by one as they are defined in the regular expression, and they will end with the callback function (which we do not need to use): `(arg1, arg2, arg3, callback) ->`.

The second `When` function needs to wait for the DOM to load before acting on it. To do this, we will use the `waitForExist` and `waitForVisible` functions. If the elements do not render, then the test will fail due to a timeout in this function. Remember that if you ever want to see what the test is doing, you can browse to your mirror.

You can find a full list of the available webdriver functions at `http://webdriver.io/api.html`, but here is a list of the ones you will use the most:

Function	Use
`waitForExist(selector[,timeout,reverse])`	Default timeout: `500`, reverse: `false`. This waits for an element to render on the DOM. Setting the `reverse` flag to `true` will instead wait for the element to stop existing.
`waitForVisible(selector[,timeout,reverse])`	Default timeout: `500`, reverse: `false`. This waits for an element to be visible (checks that the display CSS property is not set to any, that the element is not outside the viewport, and that the `opacity` CSS property is not set to `0`). Setting the `reverse` flag to `true` will instead wait for the element to be invisible.

`click(selector)`
 	
 `doubleClick(selector)`
 	
 `leftClick(selector)`
 	
 `rightClick(selector)`
	This clicks an element. Can take in a CSS selector.

`setValue(selector,values)`
 	
 `addValue(selector,values)`
	This sends a sequence of keystrokes to an element. Can use unicode characters as well to simulate things such as backspace and arrow keys. The `addValue` function will append to a set value.

Function	Use

`getText(selector)`
 	
`getValue(selector)`
	This gets the node text or input value.

`getCssProperty(selector,property)`
 	
`getAttribute(selector,attribute)`
	This gets data on a CSS property or DOM element attribute. The `property` variable will return an object instead of a string.

`then(function(valueFromGet))`	This uses data obtained from any `get` function. The first parameter is always the value of the `get` function.

Now let's build our `Then` function and use **Chai** to evaluate that everything proceeded as expected:

```
# /tests/cucumber/features/cart/step_definitions/steps.coffee
```

```coffee
do ->
  'use strict'

  module.exports = ->
    ...

    @Then /^I should have one product with quantity one in my
    cart$/, ->
      @browser
        .waitForVisible ".order_detail"
        .getText ".order_detail:nth-child(1) .quantity"
        .then (quantity) >
          expect quantity
            .to.equal "1"
```

Here, we have used the `then` function to work with the value from the `.quantity` node. We use Chai to check whether the value obtained is correct. The list of Chai functions is long, and you will find yourself using most of them. They are easy to guess though! You can find all of these functions here: `http://chaijs.com/api/bdd`.

Unit tests

Unit tests are much easier to build than behavior tests. These tests make sure that only a section of the web application is working correctly, such as `Meteor.method` or a template helper.

Unit tests make it quicker to find bugs in broken behavior tests. They should be used mostly in parts that you know can break easily, such as a publisher or a particular helper.

To run unit tests, we are going to use the `sanjo:jasmine` package:

```
meteor add sanjo:jasmine
```

Now create two directories: `/jasmine/client/integration` and `/jasmine/server/integration`. These are the special directories where `jasmine` runs tests. Let's build a quick test for the `products` publisher:

```coffee
# /tests/jasmine/client/integration/publishers/products_pub_test.
coffee

do ->
  'use strict'

  describe "Products publisher", ->
    it "should return product data", ->
      # SETUP
      subscription = Meteor.subscribe("products")

      if subscription.ready()
        # EXECUTE
        product = Products.findOne()

        # VERIFY
        expect product
          .not.toBeUndefined()
```

Jasmine is simple. First, you use the `describe` function to describe the object of the feature, and then you use the `it` function to explain each part of the feature that should work. It is common to divide the evaluating function into three blocks: SETUP, EXECUTE and VERIFY. At setup, we make sure that everything is ready for the test to run, then we execute a series of functions, and finally, we use the Chai expressions to verify whether the test passes or fails.

Unit tests are great for testing peculiarities in your code that users might not see reflected visually. Have a look at the Jasmine documentation at `http://jasmine.github.io/2.3/introduction.html` for a collection of great examples.

Summary

In this chapter, we learned how to build simple tests for our web application. In addition, we learned that they are a crucial part of the development process in order to maintain the application in both a team and nonteam setting. Behavior tests are the tests that make sure that the application is running all the features as expected, while unit tests are the tests that make sure that only particular weak spots are running as expected. Be careful with testing. While it is important to keep tests active for maintenance, it is more important to focus on the programming of the product. If you do not have time to write a full behavior test, write at least one unit test on a function that is critical for the web application to work.

In the next chapter, we are going to cover how to deploy our web application to a production quality server and how to identify errors produced by the application easily, once the application is running.

6
Deployment

This chapter will cover the steps needed to make our web application live. Also, you will learn how to set up an SSL certificate and how to track errors occurring in production actively. This chapter will cover the following topics:

- Setting up Modulus.io
- Setting up Compose.io
- Automatic error tracking
- Setting up an SSL certificate

Setting up Modulus

Modulus is currently the best place to host a Meteor project. Why? It is easy to set up and maintain. While there are several other services where we can obtain the same results, every single one of them requires more expertise with servers and a considerable amount of time on your end. We are not developing a server. We are developing an application.

Modulus.io provides support for sticky sessions, web sockets, and free SSL endpoints.

Keep in mind that Meteor's Galaxy hosting service is going to be released soon and will undoubtedly become the best place to host a Meteor web application. Until then, Modulus is the way to go.

Let's start by creating a free account at `http://modulus.io`:

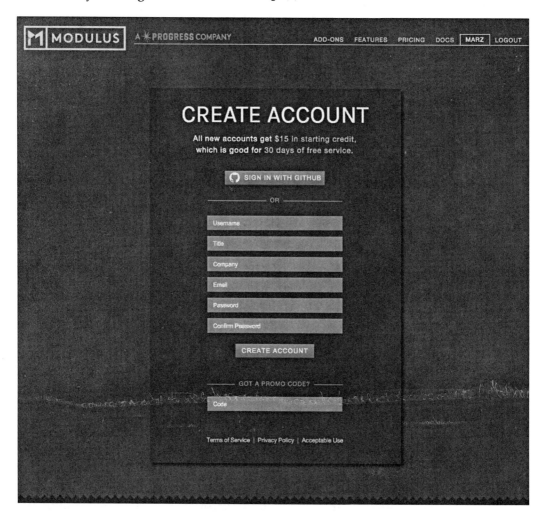

Next, you need to install the `demeteorizer` tool and the `modulus CLI` tool. Run the following commands in your terminal:

```
npm install -g demeteorizer
npm install -g modulus
```

This did not work! If your `npm install` command fails, then you need to install `node` and `npm`.

To make sure that we install `npm` properly, we need to add `homebrew` first. Install this by running this command:

```
ruby -e "$(curl -fsSL https://raw.githubusercontent.com/Homebrew/install/
master/install)"
```

Once this is done, run this command:

```
brew install node
```

When this command finishes installing everything, we will have both `node` and `npm` available globally from our command line.

Now we can install both `demeteorizer` and `modulus` easily:

```
npm install -g demeteorizer
```

```
npm install -g modulus
```

Excellent. Now we have all the tools that we need. Let's create a new project (if you want to feel like a pro, you can use the CLI too):

Make sure to select **Node.JS** as the runtime environment for the project and set the size of memory of the servo to **192MB**. If you find there is a lot of traffic coming in, you can increase the memory of the server at any time to scale your application easily.

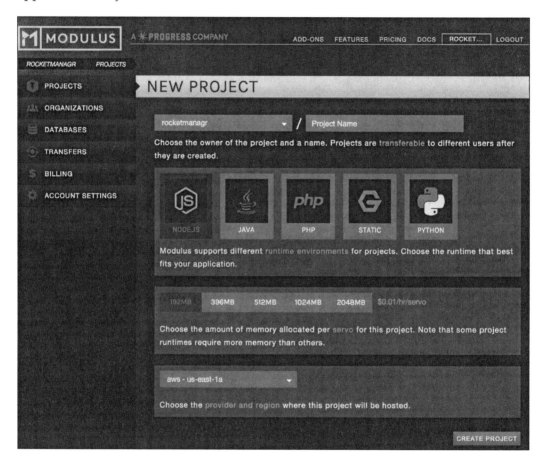

Once you have created your servo, go to the **ADMINISTRATION** tab:

Now copy the URL that has been generated for the project found next to the **Your Project URL** text:

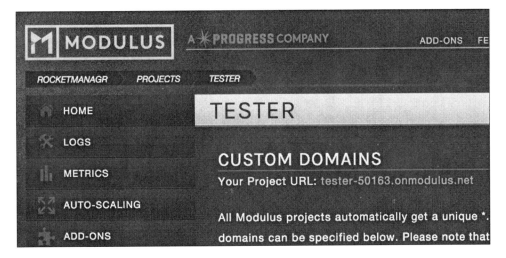

Scroll all the way to the end of the page to the **ENVIRONMENT VARIABLES**. The first thing that we need to do is set the `ROOT_URL` environment variable. Paste the project URL here. Make sure it has the `https` protocol. Here, we are taking advantage of Modulus' secure SSL endpoint. The `wizonesolutions:canonical` package will make sure that all routes will hit our `ROOT_URL`:

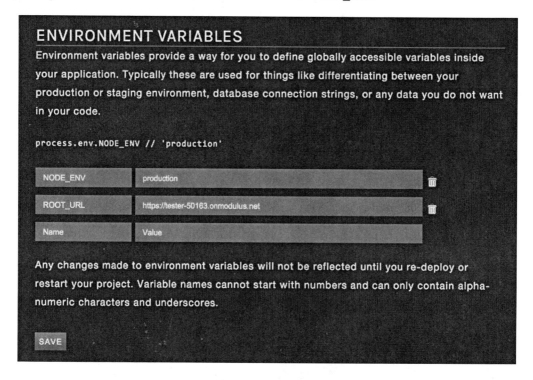

Next, we need to set up our database. We cannot deploy this yet because the application is not aware of where it is supposed to save information.

Setting up Compose

Although Modulus.io offers MongoDB hosting, Modulus does not grant access to Meteor's **oplog tailing** feature and does not have any support for multiple replica sets. Both these features are must-haves for production and this is why.

A MongoDB Replica Set is an exact copy of your database. When you first create a database in Compose, you are automatically given a primary Replica Set with a secondary Replica Set to support it. Since failures happen, the secondary Replica Set exists to replace the primary replica set immediately when the primary fails. In the database world, this is known as data redundancy.

This layer of security adds an interesting problem; how do the secondary databases know about the changes that are happening to the primary? The operations log, or oplog for short, is a special collection that Mongo uses to record all the changes that are being made to the database. These changes are read by the Replica Sets to reflect all necessary changes.

Great, now let's understand how Meteor uses the oplog. Meteor's default `poll` and `diff` method of watching changes in the database is slow. It works by comparing changes between the database and the client every 10 seconds. This creates multiple unnecessary hits on your database by default and is not fast (since a change can occur 9 seconds before Meteor looks for changes) as well. To make Meteor perform better, the Meteor team tapped into Mongo's oplog. By listening for changes in Mongo's oplog, Meteor knows exactly when and which changes to push to the client. This is called oplog tailing.

Oplog tailing drastically improves Meteor's reactivity performance by effectively tailing Mongo's operations log. It is guaranteed that a production app will not run smoothly without taking advantage of this feature.

Create your account with `compose.io`:

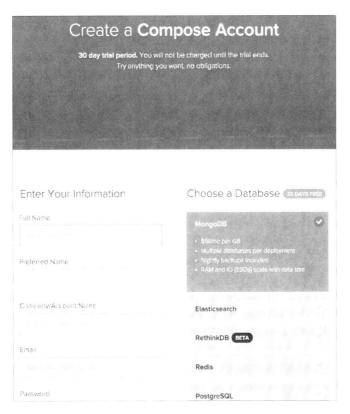

Now create a new MongoDB:

Now click the **Users** tab. Here, we need to add a user that will have access to the database and the oplog. This is the user that Modulus will use. In the following example, we are setting the user to root, the password to root, and oplog access to true:

Click on the **Admin** tab. Copy the database URI that you see displayed under **Replica Set URI**:

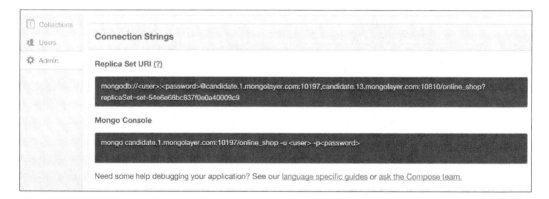

Notice the <user> and <password> sections of the string. We are going to replace these fields with the user credentials that we had defined previously.

Go back to Modulus.io and visit the project's **ADMINISTRATION** page. Scroll to the **ENVIRONMENT VARIABLES** section. Here, we need to add the URI that we had just copied in to two different variables: MONGO_URL and MONGO_OPLOG_URL.

The MONGO_URL will look like this:

```
mongodb://root:root@candidate.1.mongolayer.com:10197,candidate.13.
mongolayer.com:10810/online_shop
```

Notice that you can remove the query parameters (anything after and including the question mark).

The MONGO_OPLOG_URL will look like this:

```
mongodb://root:root@candidate.1.mongolayer.com:10197,candidate.13.
mongolayer.com:10810/local?authSource=online_shop
```

Notice that we have modified the information after the trailing slash to /local?authSource=online_shop where online_shop is the name of the database.

Excellent! This is the last time we will have to configure anything for our project's deployment. Now we can use the modulus CLI to deploy.

Go to your terminal and run the following command to log in to your user:

```
modulus login
```

If you use your GitHub account to create your Modulus account, then pass the github flag:

```
modulus login --github
```

Follow the instructions on the command line. Once you are logged in, you will need to make sure that you are in your Meteor project's root directory (where you run the Meteor command). From here, run the following command to deploy to your new server:

```
modulus deploy
```

Modulus will ask which project you want to deploy to and begin. What does Modulus do? It first identifies that the project is a Meteor project, then it runs **demeteorizer** to convert the project into a common Node.js app. This app is then deployed to the server and automatically initiated.

Setting up Kadira

Perfect! Now that we can deploy production quality web applications, we need to understand how to identify issues with them. This is where kadira.io comes into the picture. Kadira is a Meteor-specific performance and error-monitoring tool. It will collect Meteor.Errors triggered on both the client and the server. It will also show performance data for publishers and subscribers.

Kadira does this and more, and the starting plan is completely free. Let's begin by signing up. After you have signed up, you need to create a new app:

Decide a name for the app, and enter the same in the field, and click on **Create App**:

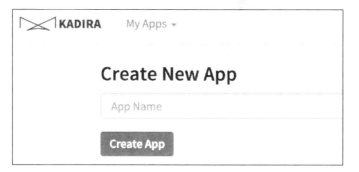

Once created, you will see a view like this:

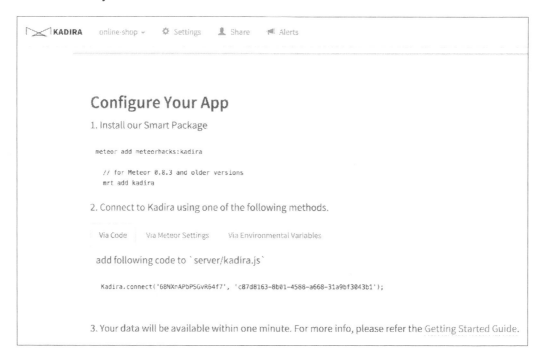

To finish, you will need to copy the code in step 2 and install the
`meteorhacks:kadira` and `meteorhacks:zones` packages:

```
meteor add meteorhacks:kadira
```

```
meteor add meteorhacks:zones
```

The `meteorhacks:zones` package improves the description of the errors from the
client side. Kadira will take advantage of this package automatically. It is important
to note that the `meteorhacks:zones` package is optional because it is still in
active development and can cause strange behavior in Meteor. Now, let's create a
configuration file for Kadira:

```
# /_globals/server/kadira.coffee

if process.env.NODE_ENV is "production"
  Kadira.connect 'appId', 'secret'
```

We are done! With this simple configuration, we can now easily track application
errors and more on Kadira:

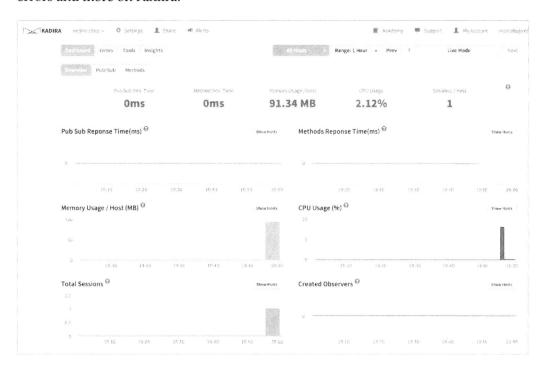

You will notice the **Errors** tab on the top-left side of the screen. This tab will show us
a list of all the errors that will occur in our application. Have a look at `meteorhacks`
and their academy to learn more about optimizing your Meteor web application.

Setting up an SSL certificate

SSL, or **Secure Sockets Layer**, is a technology that creates an encrypted connection between clients and the server. This is necessary if we want to ensure that the data transferred to our server is encrypted; this includes data such as credit card information.

Setting up SSL can be painful because it requires some command-line knowledge. We like to buy our SSL certificates from `https://www.namecheap.com/` because they are cheap and they get the job done.

The cheapest SSL certificate that you can get is **PositiveSSL**; you can find the offering at this endpoint: `https://www.namecheap.com/security/ssl-certificates/single-domain.aspx`.

After buying the certificate, you will need to generate a **Certificate Signing Request (CSR)**. Let's do this. You will be first redirected to your **Purchase Summary**. Click on **Manage**:

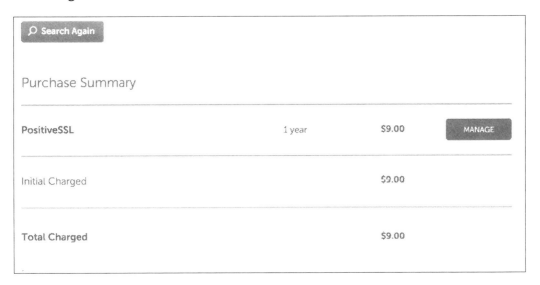

Now click **Activate Now** and leave the window open:

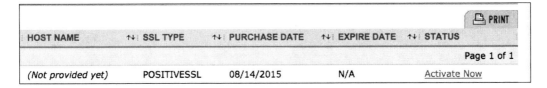

Next, open up a terminal at your project directory, and create a /.csr directory by running:

```
mkdir .csr

cd .csr
```

Now, let's use openssl to create our CSR. Run this command:

```
openssl req -nodes -newkey rsa:2048 -keyout private.key -out server.csr
```

This will give you a prompt for your site contact information; all the information fields must be filled out with your company or your information. The most important field is the **Common name** field, which must be www.yourdomain.com. Including the www will secure both www.yourdomain.com and yourdomain.com.

The command has created a private.key file and a server.csr file; you can check this by running:

```
ls
```

Keep private.key somewhere safe! You will need this later. Now open the server.csr file with any text editor such as Sublime, Atom, or, if you prefer something more basic, you can use nano or vim. You can view the contents of the current directory folder by running:

```
open .
```

Copy all the text in this file. This should look like this:

```
-----BEGIN CERTIFICATE REQUEST-----
A bunch of letters and numbers
-----END CERTIFICATE REQUEST-----
```

Go to namecheap, and change the select box to **Other** and paste the CSR to
namecheap's **Enter csr** textarea field. This should look like this:

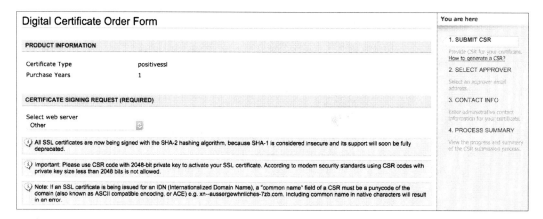

Now fill out the approver information:

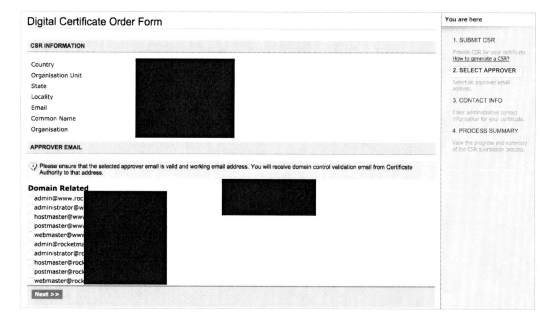

Make sure that the e-mail you select is active and under your control! If you cannot receive e-mails from the e-mail that you have selected, you will not be able to apply the SSL certificate to your webapp! In the next screen, simply submit your order and wait for the **SSL Certificate Validation** e-mail to arrive:

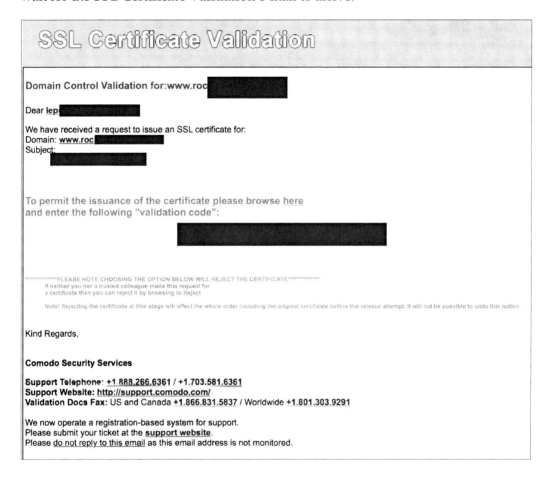

Copy your validation code, and click on the **here** link in the e-mail. This will take you to another site where you need to paste the validation code you copied and click on **Next**:

Close the window, and wait until you receive a new e-mail with a ZIP file. Download the ZIP file and unzip it. This will contain four files: `AddTrustExternalCARoot.crt`, `COMODORSAAddTrustCA.crt`, `COMODORSADomainValidationSecureServerCA.crt`, and `www_yourdomain_com.crt`.

Now, we need to use these files to create a Certificate Authority Bundle for Modulus. This is, basically, a concatenated version of all our certificates. Generate this by issuing this command in your command line where the certificates are located:

```
cat www_yourdomain_com.crt COMODORSADomainValidationSecureServerCA.crt
COMODORSAAddTrustCA.crt AddTrustExternalCARoot.crt > certificate_bundle.
crt
```

This command will produce a new `certificate_bundle.crt` directory with all the certificates concatenated.

Now browse to the Modulus.io administration page; make sure that you have already pointed your custom URL to your instance of Modulus by adding your domain name to the custom domains list. Click on the plus icon:

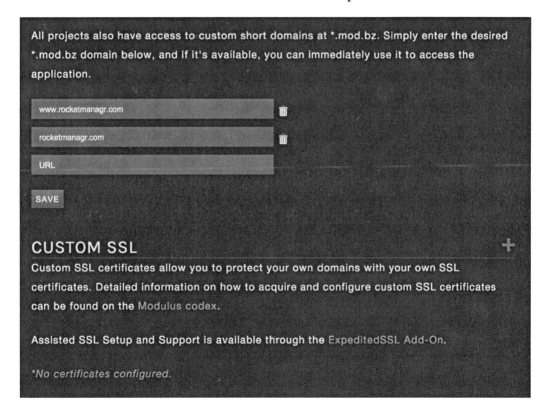

Now open the `private.key` file that was generated together with the CSR, and copy the entire text inside the file. Paste the information to the **Private Key** textarea. Then open the `certificate_bundle.crt` file, copy the information here, and paste it to the **Certificate** textarea:

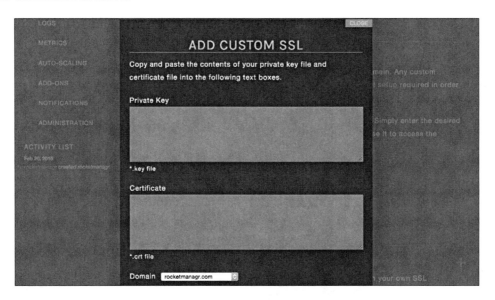

Make sure to point your certificate to the `www` domain and the `non-www` domain.

Now to complete the process, we need to make sure that the `wizonesolutions:canonical` package routes traffic to the secured domain. Scroll to the **ENVIRONMENT VARIABLES** section, and replace `ROOT_URL` with your domain starting with the `https` protocol. Your `ROOT_URL` should look like this: `https://yourdomain.com`.

You might need to restart your server to make sure that all your settings take effect. Now go to your site, and you will see that you are automatically directed to a properly secured version of your site!

Summary

This chapter is straightforward. We learned how to deploy our application to a production server hosted by modulus.io. Also, we learned how to set up our Modulus project to a production quality database server provided by Compose. We chose Compose over Modulus because we can set up oplog tailing for Meteor through it. To help us track application errors, we installed Kadira. Also, we learned how to set up an SSL certificate for our server to secure our site further. With this knowledge, we can build production quality web applications.

Index

helpers 10
HTML tags 8
templates 8-10
Jeet 55
Jeet grid systems, with Rupture 55, 56

K

Kadira
    setting up 147-149
key 41

L

loading indicator
    designing 80
    implementing 80, 81

M

many to many database relationship 34, 35
mapping table 34
merge box 18-20
Meta
    using 88
Meteor
    about 1
    animations, executing in 83-85
Meteor methods 72-76, 111-113
minimalism design 49
mirror 128
mixins 13
Modulus
    about 139
    setting up 139-144
Modulus.io
    URL 140
MongoDB Replica Set 144

O

one to many database relationship 31-33
one to one database relationship 30
online shop project
    about 20
    file structure 23, 24
    packages, requisites 20-22

oplog tailing feature 144
Optimistic UI 112
options 41
orders
    publishing, with details
        (one to many) 37-39

P

parameters, collection field
    allowedValues 104
    autoValue 105
    Blackbox 104
    Custom 105
    Decimal 104
    denyInsert 104
    denyUpdate 104
    Optional 104
    regEx 104
    Type 104
    Unique 105
parameters, Restivus
    apiPath 123
    enableCors 123
    Version 123
pattern functions, Meteor
    Match.Any() 113
    Match.Integer() 113
    Match.ObjectIncluding() 113
    Match.OneOf() 114
    Match.Optional() 113
    Match.Where() 114
persistent variables 61-64
PositiveSSL
    about 150
    reference link 150
Prerender.io 86, 87
products
    publishing, with images (one to one) 36, 37
products (many to many)
    tag, publishing with 39-41

R

ReactiveVar variables 65-72
relations
    publishing with 35

W

Thank you for buying
Meteor Design Patterns

About Packt Publishing

Packt, pronounced 'packed', published its first book, *Mastering phpMyAdmin for Effective MySQL Management*, in April 2004, and subsequently continued to specialize in publishing highly focused books on specific technologies and solutions.

Our books and publications share the experiences of your fellow IT professionals in adapting and customizing today's systems, applications, and frameworks. Our solution-based books give you the knowledge and power to customize the software and technologies you're using to get the job done. Packt books are more specific and less general than the IT books you have seen in the past. Our unique business model allows us to bring you more focused information, giving you more of what you need to know, and less of what you don't.

Packt is a modern yet unique publishing company that focuses on producing quality, cutting-edge books for communities of developers, administrators, and newbies alike. For more information, please visit our website at www.packtpub.com.

About Packt Open Source

In 2010, Packt launched two new brands, Packt Open Source and Packt Enterprise, in order to continue its focus on specialization. This book is part of the Packt Open Source brand, home to books published on software built around open source licenses, and offering information to anybody from advanced developers to budding web designers. The Open Source brand also runs Packt's Open Source Royalty Scheme, by which Packt gives a royalty to each open source project about whose software a book is sold.

Writing for Packt

We welcome all inquiries from people who are interested in authoring. Book proposals should be sent to author@packtpub.com. If your book idea is still at an early stage and you would like to discuss it first before writing a formal book proposal, then please contact us; one of our commissioning editors will get in touch with you.

We're not just looking for published authors; if you have strong technical skills but no writing experience, our experienced editors can help you develop a writing career, or simply get some additional reward for your expertise.

open source*
community experience distilled

PUBLISHING

Getting Started with Meteor.js
JavaScript Framework
Second Edition

ISBN: 978-1-78528-554-7   Paperback: 138 pages

Learn to develop powerful web applications in
minutes with Meteor

1. Learn one of the most up-to-date JavaScript
   platforms, with easy to follow, step-by-step
   instructions.

2. Familiarize yourself with Meteor's new and
   improved features.

3. Create dynamic, multi-user applications
   in JavaScript.

Learning Meteor Application
Development [Video]

ISBN: 978-1-78439-358-8   Duration: 01:52 hours

An informative walkthrough for creating a complete,
multi-tier Meteor application from the ground up

1. Master the fundamentals for delivering clean,
   concise Meteor applications with this friendly,
   informative guide.

2. Implement repeatable, effective setup and
   configuration processes and maximize your
   development efficiency on every project.

3. Utilize cutting-edge techniques and templates
   to reduce the complexity of your applications
   and create concise, reusable components.

Please check **www.PacktPub.com** for information on our titles

Meteor Cookbook

ISBN: 978-1-78328-029-2   Paperback: 364 pages

Over 65 hands-on recipes that cover every aspect of building and deploying elegant, full-stack web applications with Meteor

1. Save time and effort while fully leveraging the entire Meteor technology stack.

2. Quickly reference and implement the most powerful and useful features of one of the hottest and fastest growing JavaScript frameworks.

3. Master cutting-edge techniques used by the experts to build elegant, robust applications.

Building Single-page Web Apps with Meteor

ISBN: 978-1-78398-812-9   Paperback: 198 pages

Build real-time apps at lightning speed using the most powerful full-stack JavaScript framework

1. Create a complete web blog from frontend to backend that uses only JavaScript.

2. Understand how Web 2.0 is made by powerful browser-based applications.

3. Step-by-step tutorial that will show you how fast, complex web applications can be built.

Please check **www.PacktPub.com** for information on our titles

CPSIA information can be obtained
at www.ICGtesting.com
Printed in the USA
FSOW02n1859090817
37402FS